PRAISE FOR *THE RE*

Ronald Reagan and his advisers wag∙   ∙ing
Soviet Union – and each other – in th∙   ∙ry.
-- **Kirkus Reviews**

The Reagan Files ... is a rich collection of declassified letters, transcripts
and National Security Council meeting minutes gleaned from the Reagan
Library concerning U.S.-Soviet relations and the end of the Cold War.
-- **Steven Aftergood, Secrecy News**

Did Ronald Reagan Win the Cold War? Jason Saltoun-Ebin has spent nine
years at the Reagan Presidential Library and other archives finding the
original documents and Oval Office notes that take us as close as we are
likely to come to answering one of the great questions of the twentieth
century.
-- **Richard Reeves, bestselling author of books on Kennedy, Nixon and**
Reagan.

The Reagan Files provides fascinating new material about the decision-
making process of the Reagan presidency in the final years of the Cold
War. The book takes the reader through the original letters, meetings and
policy documents that chronicle the era, compiled with great energy and
dedication by Jason Saltoun-Ebin.
-- **David E. Hoffman, Pulitzer Prize-winning author of *The Dead Hand:***
The Untold Story of the Cold War Arms Race and Its Dangerous Legacy.

Jason Saltoun-Ebin has painstakingly assembled an invaluable collection
of documents that provide new insight into the quest for national security
during the Reagan years. Bravo!
-- **Laura Kalman, professor of history, University of California Santa**
Barbara, and author of *Right Star Rising: A New Politics, 1974-1980.*

JUL - - 2013

DEAR MR. PRESIDENT...

REAGAN/GORBACHEV

&

The Correspondence that

Ended the Cold War

EDITED AND ANNOTATED BY

JASON SALTOUN-EBIN

Visit The Reagan Files at www.thereaganfiles.com

First published in the United States by Jason Saltoun-Ebin, February 6, 2013.

ISBN-13 978-1453825655
ISBN-10: 1453825657
BISAC: History / United States / 20th Century

Cover Photo: Ronald Reagan Presidential Library.
President Reagan and General Secretary Gorbachev at the Hofdi House. Reykjavik, Iceland. October, 1987.

.

For my father, Joseph M. Ebin

<u>CONTENTS</u>

INTRODUCTION

RONALD WILSON REAGAN, the 40th president of the United States, went to sleep in the white house master bedroom on the night of March 10, 1985 unaware that relations between the United States and the Soviet Union were about to take a dramatic turn for the better. In Moscow, Konstantin Chernenko, the general secretary of the Soviet Union, lay dying in bed. Although his successor had yet to be chosen, since news of Chernenko's ill health had surfaced months before, western leaders like Prime Minister Margaret Thatcher were quietly hoping that Mikhail Gorbachev, a young soviet reformer who had skyrocketed up the communist party ladder, would be made the next general secretary of the Soviet Union.

The significance of Chernenko's death was lost on the 40th president. Reagan's diary entry for March 11, 1985 simply noted that he was woken at 4 AM and told of Chernenko's death. In the days that followed, Reagan, in his own words, "decided not to waste any time in trying to get to know the new Soviet leader."[1] Perhaps more than anything, Chernenko's death frustrated the 40th president. "How am I supposed to get anyplace with the Russians if they keep dying on me," Reagan asked his wife upon hearing the news.[2]

Never did Reagan imagine that Chernenko's death would later be seen as a turning point in the Cold War. Instead of electing another septuagenarian on his death bed, the leaders of the Soviet Union, perhaps echoing Reagan's frustration, realized they might never get anywhere with the Americans if their leaders kept dying on them. So they went for change, which came in the form of 54-year-old Mikhail Gorbachev, the youngest member of the Soviet Politburo and the first general secretary of the Soviet Union born after the Russian Revolution.

If change is what the Politburo wanted, Gorbachev did not disappoint. "In Gorbachev we have an entirely different kind of leader in the Soviet Union than we have experienced before," Secretary of State George Shultz remembered telling Vice President George H. W. Bush after the two met

---

[1] Ronald W. Reagan, *The Reagan Diaries*, (Harper Perennial, 2009), 307; Ronald W. Reagan, *An American Life,* (Simon & Schuster: NY, 2011), 612.
[2] Ronald W. Reagan, *An American Life,* (Simon & Schuster: NY, 2011), 611.

with Gorbachev following Chernenko's state funeral.[3] The CIA concurred: "In his first 100 days," according to a top-secret CIA memorandum, "Gorbachev has demonstrated...that he is the most aggressive and activist Soviet leader since Khrushchev."[4]

Reagan was far from convinced. "I can't claim that I believed from the start that Mikhail Gorbachev was going to be a *different* sort of Soviet leader," Reagan wrote in his autobiography. "Instead...I was wary."[5] Reagan was right to be wary. It was his job to protect Americans, and in 1985 no threat to American interests seemed to be greater than of Soviet efforts for world domination. Some in the CIA concurred, telling the president that Gorbachev and those around him are "not reformers and liberalizers either in Soviet domestic or foreign policy."[6]

Time has shown that those who questioned Gorbachev's sincerity were wrong. The openings of the Soviet archives have shown that Gorbachev was not out for Soviet world domination. Instead, his ascendency to general secretary signified that the Soviet Union would be contracting, not expanding as the CIA originally thought. Gorbachev's rise to power meant the Soviet Union would no longer try to keep pace with the American military industrial complex. Instead of focusing on spreading ideology, the Soviet Union would now be focusing on reforming communist ideology at home. Nuclear weapons could now be reduced, Soviet thinking probably went, because 30,000 active nuclear warheads would hardly make them any safer than 100 if they now believed a nuclear war could not be won and would not be fought.

---

[3] George P. Shultz, *Turmoil and Triumph: My Years as Secretary of State,* (Scribners: New York, 1993), 532.

[4] The CIA memorandum, titled "Gorbachev, the New Broom," was released as part of the Reagan Library's Nov. 2, 2012 event, "Ronald Reagan: Intelligence and the End of the Cold War." The document is online at: http://www.foia.cia.gov/Reagan.asp

[5] Ronald Reagan, *An American Life: An Autobiography*, (Simon & Schuster: New York, 2011), 614. Reagan also wrote in his diary: "Met with our Ambassador to the Soviet Union, Art Hartman. He confirms what I believe, that Gorbachev will be as tough as any of their leaders. If wasn't a confirmed ideologue, he never would have been chosen by the Politburo." *See* Reagan, *An American Life,* 614.

[6] Casey note to Reagan, June 27, 1985. *See* Robert Gates, *From the Shadows: The Ultimate Insider's Story of Five Presidents and How They Won the Cold War,* (Simon & Schuster, 1997), p. 332; David E. Hoffman, *The Dead Hand: The Untold Story of the Cold War Arms Race and Its Dangerous Legacy*, (Doubleday, 2009), 191.

Reagan, in 1985, just could not accept Gorbachev's claims without action, and made a Soviet withdrawal from Afghanistan a requirement for improved U.S.-Soviet relations. It was no different in arms control negotiations. Whereas Gorbachev practically threw the kitchen sink at Reagan in exchange for sweeping nuclear arms reduction treaties, Reagan's continued fear of Soviet expansion prevented him from accomplishing one of his life-long goals: the elimination of nuclear weapons.

Reagan and Gorbachev were treading in new territory. The Cold War was not like the first or second world wars. The advent of nuclear weapons had changed the paradigm of "winner take all." Nuclear weapons provided cover for the Soviet Union to abandon the Cold War without surrendering. At the same time Reagan likely did not realize that the United States could win the Cold War without a Soviet surrender. Even if Reagan thought the Soviet's were in fact retreating, his experiences in the first and second world war, like his characterization of détente as an opportunity for the Soviet Union to secretly rearm, meant nothing more than an opportunity for the U.S. to step up the offensive to deliver an overdue knock out punch to the Soviet enemy.

How was Reagan then to respond to Gorbachev's calls for the complete elimination of nuclear weapons if he could not recognize that the Soviet Union was bowing out of the Cold War? How could he agree to negotiate away the one thing (nuclear weapons) that he believed had kept the United States from finding itself fighting a third world war?

Historians, sociologists, and political scientists, continue to debate the impact that individuals can have on their time period. In looking at the period 1985-1989, specifically the overlapping of Reagan's second term with the rise to power of Mikhail Gorbachev, and the almost immediate easing of tensions between the Soviet Union and the United States, the reasons for the subsequent end of the Cold War have varied from Reagan's consistent economic pressure that allegedly bankrupted the Soviet Union to Gorbachev's internal reforms that allowed for private ownership and governmental transparency. Many have argued that Reagan single-handedly won the Cold War. Others that Gorbachev deserves all the credit.

The pages that follow tell a different story. Instead of Reagan's economic pressure and massive defense spending that bankrupted the Soviet Union, or Gorbachev's internal reforms that westernized the Soviet Union, the letters published here (many for the first time) show that Reagan's and Gorbachev's willingness to challenge forty years of Cold

War ideology (not to mention the pressure each must have felt from their own advisers) and trust each other, more than anything else, led to the easing of tensions and the eventual end of the Cold War.

Above all, this is the story of how an old hard-line anti-Communist president of the United States and a young Soviet reformer discovered that, despite their vast differences, all they needed to do was find one common area of agreement to change the world. The total elimination of nuclear weapons became their focus. Although they argued to death over the Strategic Defense Initiative, human rights issues, and proxy wars in Afghanistan, Africa and Central America, the two leaders would still come back together to focus on moving towards the complete elimination of nuclear weapons.

Reagan's first letter to Gorbachev extended an invitation to the new Soviet leader to come to Washington so they could meet and discuss issues like working towards the elimination of nuclear weapons. Gorbachev's formal response, on March 24, agreed to a summit "to search for mutual understanding on the basis of equality and account of the legitimate interests of each other." Gorbachev also told Reagan that the United States and Soviet Union had to do everything in their power to avoid a nuclear war.

As the two most powerful men in the world continued to exchange letters, beliefs like avoiding nuclear war slowly morphed into concrete proposals for the reduction and then elimination of nuclear weapons. Despite their continued disagreements, they kept talking, they kept writing, and they kept meeting because they both, to their core, believed they were put on this earth at this particular time to solve the greatest problem facing mankind: preventing nuclear Armageddon.

Reagan and Gorbachev succeeded in that ultimate goal thanks to their courage to trust each other at a time when no one else thought they should. That trust, however, did not come easy for either of them. "I realize those first letters marked the cautious beginning on both sides of what was to become the foundation of not only a better relationship between our countries," Reagan reflected in his autobiography, "but a friendship between two men."[7] With the fate of a combined U.S. and Soviet population of over 500 million people at stake, word-by-word, Reagan and Gorbachev slowly overcame their fears. One-on-one meetings, first in

---

[7] Reagan, *An American Life,* 612.

Geneva, then Reykjavik, Washington, and Moscow, certainly helped, but each of those meeting would never have taken place without the trust each leader gained in the other through their private correspondence.

Chapter 1

The Road to Geneva

[Just hours after Mikhail Gorbachev was sworn in as the next general secretary of the Soviet Union, Reagan took the initiative and penned this first letter to Gorbachev. Vice President George H.W. Bush, who was sent to the Soviet Union along with Secretary of State George Shultz to represent the United States at the state funeral marking the passing of former general secretary Konstantin Chernenko, had the opportunity to deliver the letter in person.

Reagan's first letter set the tone for future letters. Though formal, the American president expressed hope and optimism that the two leaders would be able to work together to build on gains Reagan had achieved with Gorbachev's predecessors.]

March 11, 1985

Dear Mr. General Secretary:

As you assume your new responsibilities, I would like to take this opportunity to underscore my hope that we can in the months and years ahead develop a more stable and constructive relationship between our two countries. Our differences are many, and we will need to proceed in a way that takes both differences and common interests into account in seeking to resolve problems and build a new measure of trust and confidence. But history places on us a very heavy responsibility for maintaining and strengthening peace, and I am convinced we have before us new opportunities to do so. Therefore I have requested the Vice President to deliver this letter to you.

I believe our differences can and must be resolved through discussion and negotiation. The international situation demands that we redouble our efforts to find political solutions to the problems we face. I valued my correspondence with Chairman Chernenko, and believe my meetings with First Deputy Prime Minister Gromyko and Mr. Shcherbitsky here in Washington were useful in clarifying views and issues and making it possible to move forward to deal with them in a practical and realistic fashion.

In recent months we have demonstrated that it is possible to resolve problems to mutual benefit. We have had useful exchanges on certain regional issues, and I am sure you are aware that American interests in progress on humanitarian issues remains as strong as ever. In our bilateral relations, we have signed a number of new agreements, and we have promising negotiations underway in several important fields. Most significantly, the negotiations we have agreed to begin in Geneva provide us with a genuine chance to make progress toward our common ultimate goal of eliminating nuclear weapons.

It is important for us to build on these achievements. You can be assured of my personal commitment to work with you and the rest of the Soviet leadership in serious negotiations. In that spirit, I would like to invite you to visit me in Washington at your earliest convenient opportunity. I recognize that an early answer may not be possible, but I want you to know that I look forward to a meeting that could yield results of benefit to both our countries and to the international community as a whole.

Sincerely,

Ronald Reagan

[Gorbachev quickly responded with a letter hand-delivered to Secretary of State Shultz on March 25 in which he agreed to a summit "to search for mutual understanding on the basis of equality and account of the legitimate interests of each other." Shultz took Gorbachev's agreement for a Summit to likely mean an August meeting in Helsinki "on the occasion of the tenth anniversary of the Conference on Security and Cooperation in Europe (CSCE) Final Act." Gorbachev also noted the importance he placed on the "exchange of letters" that had started between the two leaders.

Gorbachev's initial reply, Reagan reflected years later, "completed the first round of a correspondence between us that was to last for years and encompass scores of letters."[8]]

March 24, 1985

Dear Mr. President,

Let me first of all express gratitude for the sympathy shown by you personally on the occasion of a sad event for the Soviet people – the death of K.U. Chernenko.

We also appreciate the participation in the mourning rites in Moscow of the Vice-President of the United States Mr. George Bush and the Secretary of State Mr. George Shultz. I think that the conversation we had with them was – though it had to be brief – mutually useful and, one might say, even necessary under the current circumstances.

We value the practice of exchanges of views between the leadership of our two countries on the key issues of Soviet-American relations and the

---

[8] Reagan, *An American Life,* 612.

international situation as a whole. In this context I attach great importance to the exchange of letters, which has started between the two of us.

First of all I would like to say that we deem improvement of relations between the USSR and the USA to be not only extremely necessary, but possible, too. This was the central point that I was making in the conversation with your representatives in Moscow.

For your part, you also expressed yourself in favor of more stable and constructive relations, and we regard this positively. We have also taken note of your words about the new opportunities which are opening up now.

This being the case, the problem, as we understand it, is to give – through joint effort on the level of political leadership – a proper impetus to our relations in the direction the two of us are talking about, to translate into the language of (conduct) the mutually expressed willingness to improve relations, with account taken of the special responsibility borne by our two countries, of the objective fact that the Soviet Union and the United States of America are great powers and that relations between them are of decisive importance for the situation in the world in general.

Our countries are different by their social systems, by the ideologies dominant in them. But we believe that this should not be a reason for animosity. Each social system has a right to life, and it should prove its advantages not by force, not by military means, but on the path of peaceful competition with the other system. And all people have the right to go the way they have chosen themselves, without anybody imposing his will on them from outside, interfering in their internal affairs. We believe that this is the only just and healthy basis for relations among states. For our part, we have always striven to build our relations with the United States, as well as with other countries, precisely in this manner.

Besides, the Soviet leadership is convinced that our two countries have one common interest uniting them beyond any doubt: not to let things come to the outbreak of nuclear war which would inevitably have catastrophic consequences for both sides. And both sides would be well advised to recall this more often in making their policy.

I am convinced that given such approach to the business at hand, on the basis of a reasonable account of the realities of today's world and treating with a due respect the rights and legitimate interests of the other side, we could do quite a bit to benefit the peoples of our countries, as well as the whole world having embarked upon the road of a real improvement of relations.

It appears to us that it is important first of all to start conducting business in such a manner so that both we ourselves and others could see and feel that both countries are not aiming at deepening their differences and whipping up animosity, but, rather, are making their policy looking to the prospect of revitalizing the situation and of peaceful, calm development. This would help create an atmosphere of greater trust between our two countries. It is not an easy task, and I would say, a delicate one. For, trust is an especially sensitive thing, keenly receptive to both deeds and words. It will not be enhanced if, for example, one were to talk as if in two languages: one – for private contacts, and the other, as they say, -- for the audience.

The development of relations could well proceed through finding practical solutions to a number of problems of mutual interest. As 1 understand it, you also speak in favor of such a way.

We believe that this should be done across the entire range of problems, both international and bilateral. Any problem can be solved, of course, only on a mutually acceptable basis, which means finding reasonable compromises, the main criterion being that neither side should claim some special rights for itself or advantages, both on subjects between the two of them and in international affairs.

No matter how important the questions involved in our relations or affecting them in this or that manner might be, the central, priority area is that of security. The negotiations underway in Geneva require the foremost attention of the two of us. Obviously, we will have to turn again and again to the questions under discussion there. At this point I do not intend to comment on what is going on at the talks – they have just started. I shall say, though, that some statements which were made and are being made in your country with regard to the talks cannot but cause concern.

I would like you to know and appreciate the seriousness of our approach to the negotiations, our firm desire to work towards positive results there. We will invariably adhere to the agreement on the subject and objectives of these negotiations. The fact that we were able to agree on this in January is already a big achievement and it should be treated with care.

I hope, Mr. President, that you will find from this letter that the Soviet leadership, including myself personally, intends to act vigorously to find common ways to improving relations between our countries.

I think that it is also clear from my letter that we attach great importance to contacts at the highest level. For this reason I have a positive attitude to the idea you expressed about holding a personal meeting between us. And, it would seem that such a meeting should not necessarily be concluded by signing some major document. Though agreements on certain issues of mutual interest, if they were worked out by that time, could well be formalized during the meeting.

The main thing is that it should be a meeting to search for mutual understandings on the basis of equality and account of the legitimate interests of each other.

As to a venue for the meeting, I thank you for the invitation to visit Washington. But let us agree that we shall return again to the question of the place and time for the meeting.

Sincerely,
M. GORBACHEV

[President Reagan responded to Gorbachev on April 4. Reagan told Gorbachev that he very much appreciated the importance of continued correspondences and would soon be responding to his March 24 letter. Reagan also took the opportunity to reiterate to Gorbachev that he believed "new opportunities are now opening up in U.S.-Soviet relations....We must take advantage of them."

But Reagan did not write just to discuss improvements in U.S-Soviet relations. The President also warned Gorbachev that future U.S.-Soviet negotiations would be put in jeopardy if the Soviet Union did not take responsibility for the death of Major Arthur D. Nicholson, 37, who was shot to death on the afternoon of March 24, by a Soviet soldier while on a monitoring mission in East Germany.[9]]

April 4, 1985

Dear Mr. General Secretary,
The visit to Moscow of a congressional delegation headed by the distinguished Speaker of our House of Representatives provides an important, new opportunity for a high-level exchange of views between our two countries. I hope your meeting with the Speaker and his colleagues will result in a serious and useful discussion.
I believe meetings at the political level are vitally important if we are to build a more constructive relationship between our two countries. I believe my meetings in Washington with First Deputy Premier Gromyko and Mr. Shcherbitsky and your discussion in Moscow with Vice President Bush and Secretary Shultz both served this purpose. As you know, I look forward to meeting with you personally at a mutually convenient time. Together, I am

---

[9] Major Nicholson was one of 14 officers assigned to East Germany under a 1947 US-Soviet agreement that provided for the exchange of intelligence-gathering missions in East and West Germany. The Soviets maintain that Nicholson was trying to take photographs in a clearly marked restricted area, a charge the State Department denied. Major Nicholson's death is now considered the last casualty of the Cold War.

*confident that we can provide the important political impetus you
mentioned in your last letter for moving toward a more constructive and
stable relationship between our two countries.*

*I believe that new opportunities are now opening up in U.S.-Soviet
relations. We must take advantage of them. You know my view that there
are such opportunities in every area of our relations, including
humanitarian, regional, bilateral and arms control issues. In improving
stability there is no more important issue than arms control talks we have
jointly undertaken in Geneva. Our negotiators have very flexible
instructions to work with your negotiators in drafting agreements which
can lead to radical reductions, and toward our common goal, the
elimination of nuclear weapons.*

*In seizing new opportunities, we must also take care to avoid situations
which can seriously damage our relations. I and all Americans were
appalled recently at the senseless killing of Major Nicholson in East
Germany. In addition to the personal tragedy of this brave officer, this act
seemed to many in our country to be only the latest example of a Soviet
military action which threatens to undo our best efforts to fashion a
sustainable, more constructive relationship for the long term. I want you to
know that it is also a matter of personal importance to me that we take
steps to prevent the reoccurrence of this tragedy and I hope you will do all
in your power to prevent such actions in the future.*

*Let me close by reaffirming the value I place in our correspondence. I
will be replying in greater detail to your last letter. I hope we can continue
to speak frankly in future letters, as we attempt to build stronger relations
between ourselves and between our two countries.*

Sincerely

Ronald Reagan

[Reagan was impatient. Before giving Gorbachev the chance to respond, he
sent him another letter criticizing him for not taking responsibility for the
death of Major Nicholson. Reagan also stressed that a political resolution to
the Soviet invasion of Afghanistan was long overdue and that progress
should be made in arms control negotiations. Reagan also used the
opportunity to assure Gorbachev that the Strategic Defense Initiative had no
offensive purpose, and, therefore, the Soviet Union should not be
threatened by American research efforts to build a defense against ballistic
missiles. Reagan also explained that the United States pursued research on
strategic defense to protect everyone from the unfortunate possibility that a
"madman" may get his hands on a nuclear weapon. Reagan also insisted
that Gorbachev was "profoundly mistaken" to think that strategic defense
research could have an offensive purpose.

Moving to areas in which the United States and Soviet Union could come to a possible agreement, Reagan suggested that a global ban on chemical weapons would be an area in which they could come together. Reagan also used the opportunity to let Gorbachev know that he wanted to improve trade relations with the Soviet Union, but could not do so until after the political situation improved.

Questions to consider: Was Gorbachev correct to claim that research on strategic defense could be used for offensive purposes? Even if strategic defense research were truly defensive, could Gorbachev rightly see defense research as dangerous to international stability? In the early 1980s the United States Government paid American farmers not to farm to keep food prices stable. At the same time the Soviet people were suffering massive food shortages, which President Reagan could have alleviated through trade with the Soviet Union. Was President Reagan correct to restrict trade with the Soviet Union until improvements were made in political relations?]

April 30, 1985

Dear Mr. General Secretary,

As I mentioned in my letter of April 4, delivered by Speaker O'Neill, I have given careful thought to your letter of March 24 and wish to take this opportunity to address the questions you raised and to mention others which I feel deserve your attention. Given the heavy responsibilities we both bear to preserve peace in the world and life on this planet, I am sure that you will agree that we must communicate with each other frankly and openly so that we can understand each other's point of view clearly. I write in that spirit.

I had thought that we had agreed on the necessity of improving relations between our countries, and I welcomed your judgment that it is possible to do so. Our countries share an overriding interest in avoiding war between us, and – as you pointed out – the immediate task we face is to find a way to provide a political impetus to move these relations in a positive direction.

Unfortunately, certain recent events have begun to cast doubt on the desire of your government to improve relations. In particular, I have in mind the public retraction of the commitment made earlier by a responsible Soviet official to take steps to make sure lethal force is not used against members of the United States Military Liaison Mission in Germany.

Mr. General Secretary, this matter has importance beyond the tragic loss of life which has occurred. It involves fundamental principles which must be observed if we are to narrow our differences and resolve problems in our countries' relations. For this reason, I will give you my views in detail. The principles are those of dealing with each other on the basis of equality and reciprocity. The current Soviet position recognizes neither of these principles.

Now, I can understand that accidents occur in life which do not reflect the intention of political authorities. But when they do, it is the responsibility of the relevant political authorities to take appropriate corrective action.

For decades, members of our respective Military Liaison Missions in Germany operated pursuant to the Huebner-Malinin agreement without a fatal incident. That encouraging record was broken when an unarmed member of our mission was killed by a Soviet soldier. Our military personnel are instructed categorically and in writing (in orders provided to your commander) never to use lethal force against members of the Soviet Military Liaison Mission, regardless of circumstances. Our forces in the Federal Republic of Germany have never done so, even though Soviet military personnel have been apprehended repeatedly in restricted military areas. In fact, some Soviet officers were discovered in a prohibited area just three days before the fatal shooing of our officer and were escorted courteously and safely from the area.

The position which your Government most recently presented to us, therefore, is neither reciprocal in its effect nor does it reflect a willingness to deal as equals. Instead of accepting the responsibility to insure that members of the United States Military Liaison Mission receive the same protection as that we accord members of the Soviet Military Liaison Mission, what we see is the assertion of a "right" to use lethal force under certain circumstances, determined unilaterally by the Soviet side, and in practice by enlisted men in the Soviet armed forces.

Now I will offer no comment on the desirability of allowing subordinate officials – and indeed even rank-and-file soldiers – to make decisions which can affect relations between your great nations. If you choose to permit this, that is your prerogative. But in that case, your Government cannot escape responsibility for faulty acts of judgment by individuals acting in accord with standing orders.

I hope that you will reconsider the position your Government has taken on this matter, and take steps to see to it that your military personnel guarantee the safety of their American, British and French counterparts in Germany just as American, British, and French military personnel guarantee the safety of their Soviet colleagues. If your Government is unwilling or unable to abide by even this elementary rule of reciprocity, the conclusion we will be forced to draw will inevitably affect the prospects for settling other issues. The American people see this tragedy through the eyes of the widow and eight-year-old child. Consequently it will remain a penetrating and enduring problem until it is properly resolved.

Your letter mentioned a number of other important principles, but here too our agreement on the principle should not be allowed to obscure the fact that, in our opinion, the principle cited has not been observed on the Soviet side. For example I could not agree more with your statement that each social system should prove its advantages not by force, but by peaceful competition, and that all people have the right to go their chosen way without imposition from the outside. But if this is true, what are we to think of Soviet military actions in Afghanistan or of your country's policy of supplying arms to minority elements in other countries which are attempting to impose their will on a nation by force? Can this be considered consistent with that important principle?

Mr. General Secretary, my purpose in pointing this out is not to engage in a debate over questions on which we disagree, but simply to illustrate the fact that agreement on a principle is one thing, and practical efforts to apply it another. Since we seem to agree on many principles, we must devote our main effort to closing the gap between principle and practice.

In this regard, I am pleased to note that we both seem to be in agreement on the desirability of more direct consultation on various regional issues. That is a healthy sign, and I would hope that these consultations can be used to avoid the development of situations which might bring us to dangerous confrontations. I believe we should not be discouraged if, at present, our positions seem far apart. This is to be expected, given our differing interests and the impact of past events. The important thing is to make sure we each have a clear understanding of the other's point of view and act in a manner which does not provoke unintended reaction by the other.

One situation which has profoundly negative impact on our relations is the conflict in Afghanistan. Isn't it long overdue to reach a political resolution of this tragic affair? I cannot believe that it is impossible to find a solution which protects the legitimate interests of all parties, that of the Afghan people to live in peace under a government of their own choosing, and that of the Soviet Union to ensure that its southern border is secure. We support the United Nations Secretary General's efforts to achieve a negotiated settlement, and would like to see a political solution that will deal equitably with the related issues of withdrawal of your troops to their homeland and guarantees of non-interference. I fear that your present course will only lead to more bloodshed, but I want you to know that I am prepared to work with you to move the region toward peace, if you desire.

Above all, we must see to it that the conflict in Afghanistan does not expand. Pakistan is a trusted ally of the United States and I am sure you recognize the grave danger which would ensure from any political or military threats against that country.

Turning to another of your comments, I must confess that I am perplexed by what you meant by your observation that trust "will not be enhanced, if, for example, one were to talk as if in two languages. ..." Of course, this is true. And, if I am to be candid, I would be compelled to admit that Soviet words and actions do not always seem to us to be speaking the same language. But I know that this is not what you intended to suggest. I also am sure that you did not intend to suggest that expressing our respective philosophies or our views of actions taken by the other is inconsistent with practical efforts to improve the relationship. For, after all, it has been the Party which you head which has always insisted not only on the right but indeed the duty to conduct what it calls an ideological struggle.

However this may be, your remarks highlight the need for us to act so as to bolster confidence rather than to undermine it. In this regard, I must tell you that I found the proposal you made publically on April 7 – and particularly the manner in which it was made – unhelpful. As for the substance of the proposal, I find no significant element in it which we have not made clear in the past is unacceptable to us. I will not burden this letter with a reiteration of the reasons, since I am certain your experts are well aware of them. I cannot help but wonder what the purpose could have been in presenting a proposal which is, in its essence, not only an old one, but one which was known to provide no basis for serious negotiation. Certainly, it does not foster a climate conducive to finding realistic solutions to difficult questions. Past experience suggests that the best way to solve such issues is to work them out privately.

This brings me to the negotiations which have begun in Geneva. They have not made the progress we had hoped. It may now be appropriate to give them the political impetus about which we both have spoken. Let me tell you frankly and directly how I view them.

First, the January agreement by our Foreign Ministers to begin new negotiations was a good one. The problem has not been the terms of reference on the basis of which our negotiators met, even though one side may in some instances interpret the wording of the joint statement somewhat differently in its application to specifics. The problem is, rather, that your negotiators have not yet begun to discuss concretely how we can translate our commitment to a radical reduction of nuclear arsenals into concrete, practical agreements.

A particular obstacle to progress has been the demand by Soviet negotiators that, in effect, the United States agree to ban research on advanced defensive systems before other topics are dealt with seriously. I hope that I have misunderstood the Soviet position on this point, because, if that is the Soviet position, no progress will be possible. For reasons we have explained repeatedly and in detail, we see no way that a ban on research efforts can be verified. Indeed in Geneva, Foreign Minister Gromyko acknowledged the difficulty of verifying such a ban on research. Nor do we think such a ban would be in the interest of either of our countries. To hold the negotiations hostage to an impossible demand creates an insurmountable obstacle from the outset. I sincerely hope that this is not your intent, since it cannot be in the interest of either of our countries. In fact, it is inconsistent with your own actions – with the strategic defense you already deploy around Moscow and with your own major research program in strategic defense.

In this regard, I was struck by the characterization of our Strategic Defense Initiative which you made during your meeting with Speaker O'Neill's delegation – that this research program has an offensive purpose for an attack on the Soviet Union. I can assure you that you are profoundly mistaken on this point. The truth is precisely the opposite. We believe that it is important to explore the technical feasibility of defensive systems which might ultimately give all of us the means to protect our people more safely than do those we have at present, and to provide the means of moving to the total abolition of nuclear weapons, an objective on which we are agreed. I must ask you, how are we ever practically to achieve that noble aim if nations have no defense against the uncertainty that all nuclear weapons might not have been removed from world arsenals? Life provides no guarantee against some future madman getting his hands on nuclear weapons, the technology of which is already, unfortunately, far too widely known and knowledge of which cannot be erased from human minds.

This point seems, at one time, to have been clearly understood by the Soviet Government. I note that Foreign Minister Gromyko told the United Nations General Assembly in 1962 that anti-missile defenses could be the key to a successful agreement reducing offensive missiles. They would, he said then, "guard against the eventuality ... of someone deciding to violate the treaty and conceal missiles or combat aircraft." Not only has your government said that missile defenses are good; you have acted on this behalf as well. Not only have you deployed an operational ABM system, but you have upgraded it and you are pursuing an active research program.

Of course, I recognize that, in theory, the sudden deployment of effective defenses by one side in a strategic environment characterized by large numbers of "first-strike" weapons could be considered as potentially threatening by the other side. Nevertheless, such a theoretical supposition has no basis in reality, at least so far as the United States is concerned. Our scientists tell me that the United States will require some years of further research to determine whether potentially effective defensive systems can be identified which are worthy of consideration for deployment. If some options should at some time in the future be identified, development of them by the United States could occur only following negotiations with other countries, including your own, and following thorough and open policy debates in the United States itself. And if the decision to deploy should be positive, then further years would pass until the system could actually be deployed. So there is no possibility of a sudden, secretive, destabilizing move by the United States. During the research period our governments will have ample time to phase out systems which could pose a "first-strike" threat and to develop a common understanding regarding the place of possible new systems in a safer, more stable, arrangement. If such defensive systems are identified that would not be permitted by the Treaty on the Limitation of Anti-Ballistic Missile Systems, the United States intends to follow the procedures agreed upon at the time the Treaty was negotiated in 1972. In particular, Agreed Statement D attached to the Treaty calls upon the party developing a system based upon other physical principles to consult with the other party pursuant to Article XIII, with a view to working out pertinent limitations which could be adopted by amendment to the Treaty pursuant to Article XIV. I presume that it continues to be the intention of the Soviet Union to abide by Agreed Statement D in the event the long-continuing Soviet program in research on directed energy weapons were to have favorable results.

I hope this discussion will assist you in joining me in a search for practical steps to invigorate the negotiations in Geneva. One approach which I believe holds promise would be for our negotiators on strategic and intermediate-range nuclear systems to intensify their efforts to agree on specific reductions in the numbers of existing and future forces, with particular attention to those each of us find most threatening, while the negotiators dealing with defensive and space weapons concentrate on measures which prevent the erosion of the ABM Treaty and strengthen the role that Treaty can play in preserving stability as we move toward a world without nuclear weapons. Proceeding in this fashion might avoid a fruitless debate on generalities and open the way to concrete, practical solutions which meet the concerns of both sides.

I believe we should also give new attention to other negotiations and discussions underway in the security and arms control field. We know that some progress has been made in the Stockholm Conference toward narrowing our differences. An agreement should be possible this year on the basis of the framework which we have discussed with your predecessors. Specifically, we are willing to consider the Soviet proposal for a declaration reaffirming the principles not to use force, if the Soviet Union is prepared to negotiate agreements which will give concrete new meaning to that principle. Unfortunately, the response of your representatives to this offer has not been encouraging up to now. I hope that we may soon see a more favorable attitude toward this idea and toward the confidence-building measures that we and our allies have proposed.

One pressing issue of concern to us both is the use of chemical weaponry in the Iran-Iraq war. This situation illustrates the importance of curbing the spread of chemical weapons, and I suggest that it might be useful in the near future for our experts to meet and examine ways in which we might cooperate on this topic. A verifiable complete global ban on these terrible weapons would provide a lasting solution, and I would ask you therefore to give further study to the draft treaty we have advanced in the Conference on Disarmament in Geneva.

Steps to improve our bilateral relations are also important, not only because of the benefits which agreements in themselves can bring, but also because of the contribution they can make to a more confident working relationship in general.

Several of these important issues seem ripe for rapid settlement. For example, we should be able to conclude an agreement on improving safely measures in the North Pacific at an early meeting and move to discussion of civil aviations issues. We are ready to move forward promptly and open our respective consulates in New York and Kiev. Our efforts to negotiate a new exchanges agreement have, after six months, reached the point where only a handful of issues remain to be resolved. But if I had to characterize these remaining issues, I would say that they result from efforts on our side to raise our sights and look to more, not fewer, exchanges. Shouldn't we try to improve on past practices in this area? I am also hopeful that the meeting of our Joint Commercial Commission in May will succeed in identifying areas in which trade can increase substantially, but it is clear that this is likely to happen only if we succeed in improving the political atmosphere.

Finally, let me turn to an issue of great importance to me and to all Americans. As the Vice President informed you in Moscow, we believe strongly that strict observance of the Universal Declaration of Human

Rights and of the Helsinki Final Act is an important element of our bilateral relationship. Last year we suggested that Ambassador Hartman meet periodically with Deputy Foreign Minister Korniyenko to discuss confidentially how we might achieve greater mutual understanding in this area. I am also prepared to appoint rapporteurs as you suggested to the Vice President, perhaps someone to join Ambassador Hartman in such meetings. Whatever procedures we ultimately establish, I hope we can agree to try, each in accord with his own legal structure, to resolve problems in this area. If we can find a way to eliminate the conditions which give rise to public recrimination, we will have taken a giant step forward in creating an atmosphere conducive to solving many other problems.

I was glad to receive your views on a meeting between the two of us, and agree that major formal agreements are not necessary to justify one. I assume that you will get back in touch with me when you are ready to discuss time and place. I am pleased that arrangements have been made for Secretary Shultz to meet Foreign Minister Gromyko in Vienna next month, and hope that they will be able to move us toward solutions of the problems I have mentioned as well as others on the broad agenda before us.

As I stated at the outset, I have written you in candor. I believe that our heavy responsibilities require us to communicate directly and without guile or circumlocution. I hope you will give me your frank view of these questions and call to my attention any others which you consider require our personal involvement. I sincerely hope that we can use this correspondence to provide new impetus to the whole range of efforts to build confidence and to solve the critical problems which have increased tension between our countries.

Sincerely,

Ronald Reagan

May 11, 1985

Dear Mr. General Secretary,

Secretary [of Commerce] Baldrige's visit to Moscow provides me the opportunity to repeat to you my desire for a more constructive working relationship between the United States and the Soviet Union. An expansion of peaceful trade can and should be an important part of an improved relationship between our countries.

I place great significance on the discussions between Secretary Baldrige and Minister Patolichev in Moscow. They are holding the first meeting of our Joint Commercial Commission in seven years, and their meeting reflects the judgment of both our governments that an expansion of our peaceful trade is now appropriate. It is my hope that their achievements will result not only in increased trade, but also in an increased desire to seek greater cooperation in areas other than trade.

I have asked Secretary Baldrige to have pragmatic discussions with Minister Patolichev, so that the meeting of our Joint Commercial Commission will result in concrete actions by both sides to expand trade where that is now possible. To leave no doubt that the United States favors the expansion of peaceful trade with the Soviet Union, I have also authorized Secretary Baldrige to join with Minister Patolichev in a public statement on the development of trade relations.

While I believe there are some actions we can take now to facilitate trade, I doubt that there can be a fundamental change in our trade relationship without parallel improvements in other aspects of our relationship. I have mentioned in my previous letters some of the areas in which improvements would contribute greatly to a climate in which a more complete development of trade and economic cooperation would be possible.

It is my hope that upon his return from Moscow Secretary Baldrige will be able to report to me that there are areas in which both our countries can benefit from commercial cooperation and that there is Soviet interest in parallel improvements in other parts of our relationship. Given such progress, I believe that the development of our trade relationship is a question in which you and I could usefully take a continuing personal interest. I will welcome any suggestions you may have in this regard.

Sincerely,
Ronald Reagan

[General Secretary Gorbachev responded to President Reagan's eleven-page letter of April 30 with a ten-page letter on June 10. Reagan's letters had clearly put Gorbachev on the defensive. The Soviet leader immediately criticized Reagan for continued research and development of strategic defenses. Gorbachev was equally critical of Reagan's support for Pakistan, claiming that the United States was making it more difficult for the Soviet Union to leave Afghanistan.

Gorbachev also followed Reagan's suggestion of candor and frankness. In terms of SDI, Gorbachev could not have been clearer: "Any weapon system is evaluated by its capabilities, but not by public statements regarding its mission. ... All facts unambiguously indicate that the U.S. embarks upon the path of developing attack space weapons capable of performing purely offensive missions."

Gorbachev, as he would continue to do throughout his letters and meetings with Reagan, was also deeply upset that the United States accused the Soviet Union of human rights abuses. "[T]here should be no misunderstanding concerning the fact that we do not intend and will not conduct any negotiations relating to human rights in the Soviet Union," Gorbachev responded.

But Gorbachev did not write to dwell on the differences between the two leaders. "I note with satisfaction your words to the effect that our two countries have a common interest prevailing over other things – to avoid war," Gorbachev wrote. "I fully agree with that." In concrete terms, Gorbachev agreed with Reagan's suggestion to ban chemical weapons, but noted that the U.S. proposal is "inadequate" because binary weapons need to be included. He also reminded Reagan that U.S-Soviet relations have historically been fruitful when the leaders of each country "interacted." Gorbachev, like Reagan, was emphasizing the importance of dialogue even when it did not seem that there was anything to talk about.

Gorbachev concluded by reminding Reagan that he is very much in agreement that a meeting between the two leaders would be helpful, but a Washington meeting would be "unrealistic" at this time.

Questions to consider: Should Gorbachev have had more faith in Reagan when he promised that SDI research would only be used for defensive purposes? If Reagan and Gorbachev were so far apart on even the purpose of SDI, what benefit would Gorbachev and Reagan have seen from a continued dialogue? In terms of nuclear testing, Gorbachev proposed a moratorium on testing. Reagan disagreed. Why would Reagan be against banning nuclear testing? Why would Gorbachev propose a moratorium? With respect to human rights, Gorbachev asserted that the Soviet Union "would never conduct negotiations on human rights." Why would Reagan then continue to press Gorbachev on human rights? Why was Gorbachev so against any human rights negotiations?]

June 10, 1985

Dear Mr. President,

I noted the intention expressed in your letter of April 30 to share thoughts in our correspondence with complete frankness. This is also my attitude. Only in this manner can we bring to each other the essence of our respective approaches to the problems of world politics and bilateral relations. Saying this I proceed from the assumption that in exchanging views we shall look to the need to move forward on key matters, otherwise one cannot count on a turn for the better in Soviet-American relations. I understand that you agree, too, that such a turn for the better is required.

To aim at a lesser goal, say, at simply containing tensions within certain bounds and trying to make it somehow from one crisis to another – is not, in my opinion, a prospect worthy of our two powers.

We paid special attention to the fact that you share the view regarding the need to give an impetus to the process of normalizing our relations. It is not insignificant of itself. But to be candid: a number of points in your letter perplex and puzzle, and those are the points on which a special stress is made.

What I mean is the generalizations about the Soviet policy, contained in your letter, in connection with the deplorable incident with an American serviceman. As to the incident itself, we would like to hope that the explanations which were given by us were correctly understood by the American side.

Now turning to the major problems. I also believe that agreement with regard to general principles alone is not sufficient. It is important that such agreement were also reflected in the practical actions of each side. I emphasize, precisely, each side, since it clearly follows from your letter that you see disparities between the principles and practice in the actions of the Soviet Union.

It is very far from reality. There is nothing corresponding to the facts in the assertion that the USSR in its policy allegedly does not wish to conduct affairs with the U.S. on the basis of equality and reciprocity. No matter what area of our relations is taken, it transpires from a really objective assessment that it is precisely the Soviet Union that come out consistently for equality and reciprocity, does not seek advantages for itself at the expense of the legitimate interests of the U.S. And it was exactly when a similar approach was taken by the American side, too, that substantial agreements could be achieved.

It is not an accident that all agreements reached on the subject of arms limitation became possible only because the sides adhered in working them out to the principle of equality and equal security. At no point in time did the Soviet side demand more for itself. But as soon as the U.S. departed from the principle, the process of the arms limitation and reduction was ruptured. Regrettably this remains to be the case at present, too.

If, nevertheless, the question of equality and reciprocity is to be raised as a matter of principle, then it is the Soviet Union that is surrounded by American military bases stuffed also by nuclear weapons, rather than the U.S. – by Soviet bases. Try to look at the situation through our eyes, then it will become clear, who can have a real, substantiated concern.

Take then practically any issue from the sphere of our bilateral relations, whether trade, or, for example, air or sea communication. Is it that the actual state of affairs in those cases determined by the Soviet Union being against equality and reciprocity? Quite the contrary: the low level of those relations is a direct consequence of the American side's policy compatible neither with conducting affairs as equals, nor with reciprocity in the generally recognized meanings of these notions.

Or take the following aspect of the question with respect to principles and adherence to them. With regard to third countries, we impose neither our ideology, nor our social system on anybody. And do not ascribe to us what does not exist. If the question is to be raised without diplomatic contrivances as to who contributes to the international law and order and who acts in a different direction, then it appears that it is precisely the U.S. that turns out to be on the side of the groupings working against legitimate governments. And what about direct pressure on the governments whose policy does not suit the U.S.? There are enough examples of both on various continents.

I addressed these issues frankly and in a rather detailed manner not to embark upon the road of mutual recriminations, but, rather, in the hope that it will help you to understand correctly our approach to principles and their practical implementation, to appreciate our willingness to build our relations with the U.S. on the basis of equality and reciprocity in a positive and similar perception of these notions.

I think a lot about the shape the affairs between our countries can take. And I ever more firmly believe in a point I made in my previous letter: an improvement in the relations between the USSR and U.S. is possible. There is objective ground for that.

Of course, our countries are different. This fact cannot be changed. There is also another fact, however: when the leaders of both countries, as the experience of the past shows, found in themselves enough wisdom and realism to overcome bias caused by the difference in social systems, in ideologies, we cooperated successfully, did quite a few useful things both for our peoples and for all peoples. Of course, differences and different views remained, but it was our interaction that was the determining factor. And it opened up confident, peaceful vistas.

I took note of the fact that you also express yourself in favor of each social system proving its advantages in peaceful competition. Yes, we proceed from the assumption that in this competition the USSR and the U.S. will defend their ideals and moral values as each of our societies understood them. But it will result in nothing good, if the ideological struggle should be carried over into the sphere of relations between states. I believe, you understand, what I mean.

The main conclusion that naturally follows from the mutual recognition of the need for peaceful competition is that the attempts should be renounced to substitute the dispute of weapons for the dispute of ideas. One can hardly count on serious shifts in the nature of our relations so long as one side will try to gain advantages over the other on the path of the arms race, to talk with the other side from the "position of strength."

Mr. President, for understandable reasons the political leadership of both our countries must have a competent judgment regarding the existing and prospective weapons systems. It is extremely important to avoid miscalculations whose irreversible consequences will manifest themselves, if not today, then after some time.

In the past, a rigid, but at the same time quite fragile relationship was established between the nuclear weapons and anti-ballistic missile systems. The only correct conclusion was made – the Treaty of indefinite duration to limit ABM systems was concluded. It is only due to that that it became possible at all to tackle as a practical matter the problem of the limitation and reduction of nuclear weapons.

The attempts to develop a large-scale ABM system inevitably set in train a radical destabilization of the situation. Even the factor of uncertainty as such will not only prevent any limitation of nuclear weapons, but will, instead, lead to their build-up and improvement. Therefore, when we resolutely raise the question and state that the militarization of space is impermissible, it is not propaganda and not a consequence of some misunderstanding or fear of "falling behind technologically." It is a result of thorough analysis, of our deep concern about the future of relations between our countries, the future of peace.

There is also another aspect of the program of "strategic defense", which remains as if in a shadow for the broad public. But not for responsible leaders and military experts. They talk in Washington about the development of a large-scale ABM system, but in fact a new strategic offensive weapon is being developed to be deployed in space. And it is a weapon no less dangerous by its capabilities than nuclear weapons. What difference does it make, what will be used in a first disarming strike –

ballistic missiles or lasers. If there is a difference, it is that it will be possible to carry out the first strike by the new systems practically instantly.

So, from any point of view, already the beginning of the work to implement this program is destabilizing, regardless even of its final results. And it is precisely for this reason that it cannot fail to serve as an impetus to a further upswing of the arms race.

I think you will agree that in matters affecting the heart of national security, neither side can or will rely on assurances of good intentions. Any weapon system is evaluated by its capabilities, but not by public statements regarding its mission.

All facts unambiguously indicate that the U.S. embarks upon the path of developing attack space weapons capable of performing purely offensive missions. And we shall not ignore that. I must say this frankly. I ought to confess that what you have said about the approach of the U.S. to the question of the moratorium on space and nuclear weapons, enhances our concern. The persistent refusal of the American side to stop the arms race cannot but put in question the intentions of the U.S.

And what is going on at the negotiations in Geneva? The American side is trying to substitute only a part of the agreed mandate for the negotiations for the whole of it. An integral element is being removed from the really agreed formula for the negotiations – the obligation to prevent an arms race in space, to consider and resolve all issues in their interrelationship. The American side has so far done nothing to bring agreement closer. On the subject of preventing an arms race in space the U.S. delegation did not present a single consideration at all. I emphasize, not a single one. What for should after that one be surprised: why, indeed, there is no movement on the nuclear arms reduction?

I wish to mention, in passing, that the American representatives maintain – this point is also contained in your letter – that it is impossible to verify prohibition on scientific research. However, a different thing is involved: a federal program of research activities directly and specifically oriented towards the development of attack space weapons, a large-scale ABM system with space-based components. The very announcement of such a program is in clear contradiction with the ABM Treaty. (Incidentally, if one is to take the entire text of the "agreed statement" to the ABM Treaty, and not only its part which is quoted in your letter, it is easy to see that it is aimed not at weakening, but at strengthening the central provision of the treaty – dealing with the sides' renunciation of the development of large-scale ABM systems).

As to the assertions that the USSR is allegedly engaged in its own "large research program in the area of strategic defense", here, as Americans put it, apples are confused with oranges. The Soviet Union does nothing that would contravene the ABM Treaty, does not develop attack space weapons.

Thus, the question of verification is in this case a far-fetched question, if one is clearly to proceed from the premise that nothing can be done – no matter what names one can come up with for it – that is unambiguously prohibited by the ABM Treaty.

Mr. President, I would like to hope that you will have another close look at the problem of non-militarization of space, at its interrelationship with solving the problem of nuclear weapons, and from that angle – at the prospects for the Geneva negotiations. It is in this objective linkage that there lies a resolution of the problems of the limitation of nuclear arms, a real possibility to get down to their radical reduction and thereby to proceed to the liquidation of nuclear weapons as such. We shall not be able to avoid anyway having precisely the complex of these issues as a determining factor both for our relations and for the situation in the world as a whole. This follows from the special responsibility of our two countries.

I am convinced that we must and can be up to this responsibility. In this connection I note with satisfaction your words to the effect that our two countries have a common interest prevailing over other things – to avoid war. I fully agree with that.

Now, with regard to what other steps could be taken, among other things, to stimulate progress in Geneva. We are convinced that of very important – and practical significance – would be the cessation of all nuclear weapon tests. In this area a lot can be done by our two countries. Specifically, we propose the following practical steps. Putting into effect the up till now unratified Soviet-American treaties of 1974 and 1976. Coming to terms on the resumption of trilateral – with the participation of Britain – negotiations on the complete and general prohibition of nuclear weapon tests and, acting vigorously, working towards their speedy and successful conclusion. Finally, we propose that the USSR and U.S. interact in carrying out such a specific and very substantial step on the part of all nuclear powers as a moratorium on any nuclear explosions would be. We are in favor of introducing such a moratorium as soon as possible.

The problem of prohibiting chemical weapons needs to be resolved. But its resolution should be sought realistically. I must say that the positions which the U.S. has so far had on a number of important aspects of this problem, do no meet this criterion. We would like the American side to pay attention to the proposals we have put forward. We agree that bilateral consultations between our representatives would be useful, for example, within the framework of the Geneva Conference on disarmament. It should be recognized, however, that the efforts which are being made in the U.S.

for the chemical, above all, as concerns binary weapons, are not a favorable prerequisite at all for removing chemical weapons completely and forever from the military arsenals of states.

The state of things at the Stockholm Conference leaves one with an ambiguous impression. On the one hand, it would seem that there is common understanding regarding the need for an agreement on the basis of an optimum combination of major political obligations and military-technical confidence-building measures. On the other hand, the Western representatives, the American representatives first of all, clearly do not hasten to fill this understanding with specific mutually acceptable – I emphasize, mutually acceptable content. We are for having a substantial understanding, really helping to enhance confidence. Such are the instructions of our representatives. They are prepared to listen to constructive considerations which the American delegation may have. To put it briefly, we are for working towards a successful conclusion of the conference.

I would like, Mr. President to draw your attention to the negotiations on the reduction of armed forces and armaments in Central Europe. Sometimes we hear from the American representatives that our proposals made last February "stimulate interest". But it does not show at all at the negotiations themselves. It would seem that reaching agreement on initial reductions of the Soviet and American forces in that area would be in your and our interests, in the interests of a military relaxation in Europe. Could you look into it to see whether you might find it possible to advance things in this area?

One of the sources of tension in the relations between the USSR and U.S. is a difference in the assessment of what is going on in the world. It seems that the American side frequently ignores the in-depth causes of events and does not take fully into account the fact that today a great number of states operate – and most actively, too – in world politics, each with its own face and interests. All this immeasurably complicates the general picture. A correct understanding of this would help avoid serious mistakes and miscalculations.

In the past we used to have a positive experience of interaction in lowering tensions in some areas, in preventing dangerous outbreaks. But it worked this way when the readiness was shown to take into account the legitimate interests of each other and the positions of all the sides involved in a certain situation.

We positively assess the agreement of the American side to have exchanges of views on some regional problems. We expect it to accept our proposal that a wider range of regional problems be the subject of such exchanges and that those exchanges look to seeking specific ways of *settling tense situations. In this connection I took note of the readiness, expressed in your letter, to work together with the Soviet Union, so that the situation around Afghanistan would be moving toward a peaceful settlement. I would like to have a more clear understanding of how the American side is seeing it. Such an opportunity is provided by the upcoming consultations of our experts.*

However, our opinions in this matter as well will be based upon practical deeds of the U.S. From the point of view of achieving a political settlement, and not only from that point of view, we cannot accept what you say in your letter with respect to Pakistan. We perceive the behavior of that country not only as not corresponding to the goal of a political settlement around Afghanistan, but also as dangerous and provocative. We expect that the U.S., being closely linked with Pakistan and also taking into account its own interests, will exert restraining influence on it. The curtailing of its direct support to antigovernment armed formations intruding into Afghanistan from Pakistan, would be a positive signal from the American side. In other words, the U.S. has the possibilities to confirm by actions its declared readiness to achieve a political settlement around Afghanistan on the basis of a just solution of the questions connected with it and to eliminate tensions in this region as a whole. Such a mode of action will not be left unnoticed by our side and would clearly work toward straightening our Soviet-American relations.

Some kind of movement seems to be discernable in the area of strictly bilateral relations between our countries. You, evidently, have noticed that we support this trend. However, there should be no misunderstanding concerning the fact that we do not intend and will not conduct any negotiations relating to human rights in the Soviet Union. We, as any other sovereign state, regarded and will regard these questions in accordance with our existing laws and regulations. Let us, Mr. President, proceed from this in order not to aggravate additionally our relations. The development of our ties can be based only on mutual interest, equality and mutual benefit, respect for the rights and legitimate interests of each other.

We consider as positive the fact, that in some instances the once diversified structure of Soviet-American relations starts – although not very intensively, to put it outright – to be restored and to be filled with content. In particular, we consider useful the talks between our ministers of trade which took place in Moscow recently. We intend to look for mutually acceptable solutions in other areas as well, which constitute the subject of discussion between us, and to expand the range of such areas.

It is encouraging, that contacts, including those between parliaments of our two countries, have become more active recently. As I have already said to the representatives of the U.S. Congress, we live in a time, when people shaping the policy of the USSR and the U.S., must necessarily meet, have contacts with each other. To speak in broad terms, we stand for building vigorously a bridge to mutual understanding and cooperation and for developing trust.

In conclusion, I would like to confirm my positive attitude to a personal meeting with you. I understand that you feel the same way. Our point of view on this matter was outlined by Andrey A. Gromyko to Mr. Shultz during their stay recently in Vienna. As to the place for holding it, I understand there are motives which make you prefer the meeting to be held in the U.S. But I have no less weighty motives due to which, taking into account the present state of Soviet-American relations, this variant is unrealistic.

Important international problems are involved and we should use the time to search for possible agreements which could be readied for the meeting. For our part, we are entirely for this.

Sincerely,

M. Gorbachev

[Gorbachev most likely sent his June 10 letter before he had the opportunity to read the transcript of Reagan's June 10 White House Press statement, which accused the Soviet Union of not adhering to the provisions of the unratified SALT II Treaty. Reagan also announced that if the Soviet Union did not start to adhere to the SALT II provisions, the United States would no longer stay within the numerical limits agreed to in the Treaty. In essence, Reagan declared, the United States would breakout of the SALT II constraints if Soviet violations were not soon corrected.

The Soviet response was quick and to the point: "President Reagan's statement pledging continued adherence to the 1979 arms treaty confirmed his intention to destroy the entire system of arms-control accords."[10]]

[Gorbachev responded to Reagan's June 10 accusations on June 22.]

June 22, 1985

Dear Mr. President,

In connection with your letter of June 10, in which you outline the U.S. Government's decision on the SALT II Treaty made public the same day, I

---

[10] *NYT:* June 12, 1985: "Soviet's Say Reagan is Gradually Ending Pact." A8.

deem it necessary to express the viewpoint of the Soviet leadership on this matter.

I shall start by stating that your version of the past and present state of affairs in the key areas of Soviet-American relations, that of the limitation and reduction of strategic arms, cannot withstand comparison with the actual facts. Evidently, it was not by chance that you chose 1982 as your point of reference, the year when the American side declared its readiness to comply with the main provisions of the SALT II Treaty, unratified by the United States. Unfortunately, however, it was not this that determined the general course of your administration's policy and its practical actions with regard to strategic armaments.

It is hard to avoid the thought that a choice of a different kind had been made earlier, when it was stated outright that you did not consider yourself bound by the obligations assumed by your predecessors under agreements with the Soviet Union. This was perceived by others, and in the United States too, as repudiation of the arms limitations process and the search for agreements.

This was confirmed in practice: an intensive nuclear arms race was initiated in the United States. Precisely through this race, it would seem, and began to see and continues to see to this day the main means for achieving "prevailing" positions in the world under the guise of assuring U.S. national security.

In this sense, the few steps of the American side that you mentioned that went in a different direction and took account of the realities of today's world, are they not just temporary, "interim?"

It is not for the sake of polemics, but in order to restore the full picture of what has occurred, that I would like to return briefly to what has been done by the United States with regard to the current regime for strategic stability.

One cannot dispute the fact that the American side created an ambiguous situation whereby the SALT II Treaty, one of the pillars of our relationship in the security sphere, was turned into a semi-functioning document that the U.S., moreover, is now threatening to nullify step by step. How can one then talk about predictability of conduct and assess with sufficient confidence the other side's intention?

It is difficult to evaluate the damage done to our relationship and to international stability as a whole by your administration's decision to break off a process of negotiations that the USSR and the U.S. assumed a legal obligation to conduct. Such an obligation is contained in the very text of the SALT II Treaty, as well as in the accompanying "Joint Statement of Principles and Basic Guidelines for Subsequent Negotiations on the Limitation of Strategic Arms."

The chain ensuring the viability of the process of curbing the arms race, put together through great effort, was consciously broken.

Today it is especially clear that this caused many promising opportunities to slip by, while some substantial elements of our relationship in this area were squandered.

The United States crossed a dangerous threshold when it preferred to cast aside the Protocol to the SALT II Treaty instead of immediately taking up, as was envisaged, the resolution of these issues which were dealt with in the Protocol. Those issues are of cardinal importance – the limitation and prohibition of entire classes of arms. It is no secret as to what guided the American side in taking this step: it wanted to gain an advantage by deploying long-range cruise missiles. As a result, already today one has to deal with thousands of such missiles. The U.S. sought to sharply tilt in its favor the fine-tuned balance of interests underlying the agreement. Now you see, I believe, that it did not work out this way. We too are deploying cruises missiles, which we had proposed to ban. But even now we are prepared to come to an agreement on such a ban, should the U.S., taking a realistic position, agree to take such an important step.

The deployment in Western Europe of new nuclear systems designed to perform strategic missions was a clear circumvention, that is non-compliance, by the American side with regard to the SALT II Treaty. In this, Mr. President, we see an attempt by the United States, taking advantage of geographic factors, to gain a virtual monopoly on the use of weapons in a situation for which our country has no analogue. I know that on your side the need for some regional balance is sometimes cited. But even in that case it is incomprehensible why the U.S. refuses to resolve the issue in a manner which would establish in the zone of Europe a balance of medium-range missiles, whereby the USSR would not have more missiles and warheads on them than are currently in the possession of England and France. Such a formula would not infringe upon anyone's interests, whereas the distortion caused by the American missiles in Europe is not a balance at all.

In broader terms, all these violations by the United States of the regime for strategic stability have one common denominator: departure from the principle of equality and equal security. This and nothing else is the reason for the lack of progress in limiting and reducing nuclear arms over the past 4-5 years.

However, I would like you to have a clear understanding of the fact that, in practice, strategic parity between our countries will be maintained. We cannot envisage nor can we permit a different situation. The question, however, is at what level parity will be maintained – at a decreasing or an increasing one. We are for the former, for the reduction in the level of strategic confrontation. Your government, by all indications, favors the latter, evidently hoping that at some stage the U.S. will ultimately succeed in getting ahead. This is the essence of the current situation.

Should one be surprised, then, that we are conducting negotiations, yet the process of practical arms limitation remains suspended? It would probably not be too great a misfortune if this process simply remained frozen. But even that is not the case. The "star wars" program – I must tell you this, Mr. President – already at this stage is seriously undermining stability. We strongly advise you to halt this sharply destabilizing and dangerous program while things have not gone too far. If the situation in this area is not corrected, we shall have no choice but to take steps required by our security and that of our allies.

We are in favor, as you say, of making the best use of the chance offered by the Geneva negotiations on nuclear and space arms. Our main objective at those negotiations should be to reestablish the suspended process of limiting the arms race and to prevent its spread into new spheres.

The SALT II Treaty is an important element of the strategic equilibrium, and one should clearly understand its role as well as the fact that, according to the well-known expression, one cannot have one's pie and eat it too.

Your approach is determined by the fact that the strategic programs being carried out by the United States are about to collide with the limitations established by the SALT II Treaty, and the choice is being made not in favor of the Treaty, but in favor of these programs. And this cannot be disavowed or concealed, to put it bluntly, by unseemly attempts to accuse the Soviet Union of all mortal sins. It is, moreover, completely inappropriate in relations between our two countries for one to set forth conditions for the another as is done in your letter with regard to the Soviet Union.

I am saying all this frankly and unequivocally, as we have agreed.

One certainly cannot agree that the provisions of the SALT II Treaty remain in force allegedly as the result of restraint on the part of the United States. Entirely by contrary. The general attitude toward the Treaty shown by the American side and its practical actions to undermine it have given us every reason to draw appropriate conclusions and to take practical steps. We did have and continue to have moral, legal and political grounds for that.

We did not, however, give away to emotions; we showed patience, realizing the seriousness of the consequences of the path onto which we were being pushed. We hoped also that sober reasoning, as well as the self-interest of the U.S., would make the American side take a more restrained position. That was what in fact happened to a certain, though not to a full, extent. And we have treated this in businesslike fashion. Without ignoring what has been done by the American side contrary to the SALT II Treaty, we nevertheless at no time have been the initiators of politico-propagandistic campaigns of charges and accusations. We have striven to discuss seriously within the framework of the SCC the well-founded concerns we have had. We also have given exhaustive answers there to questions raised by the American side.

Unfortunately, the behavior of the other side was and continues to be utterly different. All those endless reports on imaginary Soviet violations and their publication did not and cannot serve any useful purpose, if one is guided by the tasks of preserving and continuing the process of arms limitation. Why mince words, the objective is quite different: to cast aspersions on the policy of the Soviet Union in general, to sow distrust toward it and to create an artificial pretext for an accelerated and uncontrolled arms race. All this became evident to us already long ago.

One has to note that your present decision, if it were to be implemented, would be a logical continuation of that course. We would like you, Mr. President, to think all this over once again.

In any event, we shall regard the decision that you announced in the entirety of its mutually-exclusive elements which, along with the usual measures required by the Treaty, includes also a claim to some "right" to violate provisions of the Treaty as the American side chooses. Neither side has such a right. I do not consider it necessary to go into specifics here, a lot has been said about it, and your military experts are well aware of the actual, rather than distorted, state of affairs.

One should not count on the fact that we will be able to come to terms with you with respect to destroying the SALT II Treaty through joint efforts. How things will develop further depends on the American side, and we shall draw the appropriate conclusions.

The question of the approach to arms limitation has been, is, and will be the central issue both in our relations and as far as the further development of the overall international situation is concerned. It is precisely here, above all, that the special responsibility borne by our two countries is manifested, as well as how each of them approaches that responsibility.

In more specific terms it is a question of intentions with regard to one other. No matter what is being done in other spheres of our relationship, in the final analysis, whether or not it is going to be constructive and stable depends above all on whether we are going to find a solution to the central issues of security on the basis of equality and equal security.

I would like to reaffirm that, for our part, we are full of resolve to strive to find such a solution. This determines both our attitude toward those initial limitations which were arrived at earlier through painstaking joint labor, and our approach to the negotiations currently underway in Geneva and elsewhere.

I wish to say this in conclusion: one would certainly like to feel tangibly the same attitude on the part of the United States. At any rate, as I have already had a chance to note, we took seriously the thought reiterated by you in our correspondence with regard to a joint search for ways to improve Soviet-American relations and to strengthen the foundations of peace.

Sincerely,
M. Gorbachev

[Just a few weeks after Gorbachev's June 22 letter, Reagan and Gorbachev announced that they agreed to a November summit in Geneva to make progress in arms control negotiations.

The summer continued with press statements and radio addresses on the upcoming Geneva Summit. Reagan continued to emphasize the importance he placed on SDI research. He could not, however, devote all his attention to the upcoming Geneva Summit. Reagan spent much of his time that summer dealing with how to gain the release of several American hostages held in Lebanon, including CIA Beirut Station Chief William Buckley.

Gorbachev, on a public relations tour of his own, sat down with *Time* magazine on September 3 for his first interview with western journalists. Asked about the prospects for a successful arms agreement at the Geneva Summit, Gorbachev responded that without an agreement restraining the SDI program, no other agreements would be reached.

Gorbachev was not bluffing. In his next letter to Reagan, on September 12, he proposed a 50 percent reduction in nuclear arms if Reagan agreed to "a complete ban on space attack weapons." For Europe, Gorbachev also announced, he would agree to reduce the number of Soviet warheads to whatever level of intermediate range nuclear forces Britain and France possessed. Gorbachev had successfully backed Reagan into a corner. If Reagan were really serious about arms reductions, as he had so often claimed, Gorbachev had now told the world he was willing to meet Reagan's reductions demands. Reagan had some serious thinking to do, though, because Gorbachev required that any arms reductions agreement be linked to an agreement to limit SDI research.]

September 12, 1985

Dear Mr. President:

I would like to communicate some thoughts and considerations in continuation of the correspondence between us and specifically with a view to our forthcoming personal meeting.

I assume that both of us take this meeting very seriously and are thoroughly preparing for it. The range of problems which we are to discuss has already been fairly clearly delineated. They are all very important.

Of course, the differences between our two countries are not minor and our approaches to many fundamental issues are different. All this is true. But at the same time the reality is such that our nations have to coexist whether we like each other or not. If things ever come to a military confrontation, it would be catastrophic for our countries, and for the world as a whole. Judging by what you have said, Mr. President, you also regard a military conflict between the USSR and the USA as inadmissible.

Since that is so, in other words, if preventing nuclear war and removing the threat of war is our mutual and, for that matter, primary interest, it is imperative, we believe, to use it as the main lever which can help to bring cardinal changes in the nature of the relationship between our nations, to make it constructive and stable and thus contribute to the improvement of the international climate in general. It is this central component of our relations that should be put to work in the period left before the November meeting, during the summit itself and afterwards.

We are convinced that there are considerable opportunities in this regard. My meeting with you may serve as a good catalyst for their realization. It seems that we could indeed reach a clear mutual understanding on the inadmissibility of nuclear war, on the fact that there could be no winners in such a war, and we could resolutely speak out against seeking military superiority and against attempts to infringe upon the legitimate security interests of the other side.

At the same time we are convinced that a mutual understanding of this kind should be organically complemented by a clearly expressed intention of the sides to take actions of a material nature in terms of the limitation and reduction of weapons, of terminating the arms race on Earth and preventing it in space.

It is such an understanding that would be an expression of the determination of the sides to move in the direction of removing the threat of war. Given an agreement on this central issue it would be easier for us, I think, to find mutual understanding of solutions of other problems.

What specific measures should receive priority? Naturally, those relating to the solution of the complex of questions concerning nuclear and space arms. An agreement on non-militarization of space is the only road to the most radical reductions of nuclear arms. We favor following this road unswervingly and are determined to search for mutually acceptable solutions. I think that in this field both sides should act energetically and not postpone decisions. It would be good to be able to count on having obtained some positive results by the time of my meeting with you.

In connection with certain thoughts contained in your letter of July 27 of this year, I would note that on several occasions we have explicitly expressed our views on the American program of developing space attack weapons and a large-scale anti-ballistic missile system. It is based not on emotions or subjective views, but on facts and realistic assessments. I stress once again – the implementation of this program will not solve the problem of nuclear arms, it will only aggravate it and have the most negative consequences for the whole process of the limitation and reduction of nuclear arms.

On the other hand, quite a lot could be done through parallel or joint efforts of our countries to slow the arms race and bring it to a halt, above all in its main arena – the nuclear one. It is indeed for this and no other purpose that we have taken a number of unilateral, practical steps.

Mr. President, both you and I understand perfectly well the importance of conducting nuclear explosions from the standpoint of the effectiveness of existing nuclear weapons and the development of new types of nuclear weapons. Consequently, the termination of nuclear tests would be a step in the opposite direction. This is what guided our decision to stop all nuclear explosions and appeal to the U.S. to join us in this. Please look at this issue without preconceived notions. It is quite clear that at the present level of nuclear arms our countries possess, a mutual termination of nuclear tests would not hurt the security of either of them.

Therefore, if there is a true desire to halt the nuclear arms race, then there can be no objection to a mutual moratorium, and the benefit it brings would be great. But the continuation of nuclear tests – albeit in the presence of somebody's observers – would be nothing else but the same arms race. The U.S. still has time to make the right decision. Imagine how much it would mean. And not only for Soviet-American relations.

But a moratorium on nuclear tests, of course, is still not a radical solution to the problem of preventing nuclear war.

In order to accomplish that, it is necessary to solve the whole complex of interrelated matters which are the subject of the talks between our delegation in Geneva.

It is quite obvious that in the final analysis the outcome of these talks will be decisive in determining whether we shall succeed in stopping the arms race and eliminating nuclear weapons in general. Regrettably, the state of affairs at the Geneva talks gives rise to serious concern.

We have very thoroughly and from every angle once again examined what could be done there. And I want to propose to you the following formula – the two sides agree to a complete ban on space attack weapons and a truly radical reduction, say by 50 percent, of their corresponding nuclear arms.

In other words, we propose a practical solution of the tasks which were agreed upon as objectives of the Geneva negotiations – not only would the nuclear arms race be terminated, but the level of nuclear confrontation would be drastically reduced, and at the same time an arms race in space would be prevented. As a result, strategic stability would be strengthened greatly and mutual trust would grow significantly. Such as step by the USSR and U.S. would, I believe, be an incentive for other powers possessing nuclear arms to participate in nuclear disarmament, which you pointed out as important in one of your letters.

We view things realistically and realize that such a radical solution would require time and effort. Nonetheless, we are convinced that this problem can be solved. The first thing that is needed is to have our political approaches coincide in their essence. Secondly, given such coincidence, it is important to agree on practical measures which facilitate the achievement of these goals, including a halt in the development of space attack weapons and a freeze of nuclear arsenals at their greatest quantitative levels, with a prohibition of the development of new kinds and types of nuclear weapons.

In addition, major practical measures could include the removal from alert status and dismantling of an agreed number of strategic weapons of the sides as well as mutually undertaking to refrain from the deployment of any nuclear weapons in countries which are now nuclear-free, and undertaking not to increase nuclear weapons stockpiles and not to replace nuclear weapons with new ones in the countries where such weapons are deployed.

Naturally, the issue of medium-range nuclear weapons in Europe also requires resolution. I would like to emphasize once again: the Soviet Union favors a radical solution whereby, as we proposed in Geneva, the USSR would retain in the European zone no more weapons of this type, using warheads as the unit of count, than Britain and France possess.

Our delegation at the Geneva negotiations has appropriate instructions, and it intends to present our specific proposal on this whole range of issues and to give comprehensive clarifications in the near future. We count on the positive reaction of the U.S. side and hope that it will be possible to achieve results at the present round of talks.

Meaningful practical steps could and should be taken in the area of confidence-building measures and military measures aimed at easing tensions. I have in mind, in particular, that our two countries, together with other participants of the Stockholm Conference, should make a maximum effort to work towards successful completion of the conference. Such an opportunity, it seems, has not emerged. I would like to repeat what has already been said by our Minister of Foreign Affairs to the U.S. Secretary of State – we are in favor of making the subject matter of the Stockholm conference a positive element of my meeting with you.

Whether or not an impetus is given to the Vienna talks largely depends on our two countries. During the meeting in Helsinki the Secretary of State promised that the U.S. side would once again closely look at the possibility of first reducing Soviet and American troops in Central Europe as we have proposed. I am sure that such an agreement would make a favorable impact on the development of the all-European process as well. I see no reason why it should not be in the interest of the U.S.

In proposing practical measures concerning arms limitation and disarmament we, of course, have in mind that they should be accompanied by relevant agreed verification measures. In some cases it would be national technical means, and in other cases, when it is really necessary, the latter could be used in conjunction with bilateral and international procedures.

I have not attempted to give an exhaustive list of measures to limit arms and relax military tensions. There could be other measures as well. We would listen with interest to the proposals of the U.S. side on this score. The main thing is for both sides to be ready to act in a constructive way in order to build a useful foundation, which, if possible, might also be included in the summit meeting.

Mr. President, for obvious reasons I have paid particular attention to central issues facing our countries. But of course we do not belittle the importance of regional problems and bilateral matters. I assume that these questions will be thoroughly discussed by E.A. Shevardnadze and G. Shultz with a view to bringing our positions closer and, better still, finding practical solutions wherever possible.

We hope that in the course of the meetings which our Minister of Foreign Affairs will have with you and the Secretary of State, as well as through active work at the Geneva talks, in Stockholm and in Vienna, and by means of exchanges through diplomatic channels, it will be possible in the time left before my meeting with you to create a situation making for a truly productive meeting.

We believe that the outcome of this preparatory work as well as the results of my discussions with you at the meeting itself could be reflected in an appropriate joint document. If you agree, it would be worthwhile, I think, to ask our Ministers to determine how work on such a final document could be best organized.

Sincerely,
M. Gorbachev

October 12, 1985

Dear Mr. President,

Our Minister Eduard A. Shavardnadze has informed me in detail about his conversation with you in Washington on September 27.

While there exists substantial differences in the positions of the two sides regarding concrete issues, which surfaced also in the course of that conversation and which I shall not touch upon in this letter, we deem it important that you, like us, proceed from the objective fact that we all live on the same planet and must learn to live together. It really is a fundamental judgment.

Here I would like to give you my answer only to one specific question you raised during the conversation with Eduard A. Shevardnadze, namely with regard to a confidential exchange of opinions between us bypassing, should it become necessary, the usual diplomatic channel. I am in favor of this. Indeed, there may arise the need to contact each other on matters on whose solution depend both the state of Soviet-American relations and the world situation as a whole.

On our side to maintain the confidential liaison with a person who will be designated by you for this purpose is entrusted to Ambassador Anatoly F. Dobrynin.

Sincerely,
M. Gorbachev

October 22, 1985

Dear Mr. General Secretary,

Thank you for your letter of September 12, which was delivered to me by Foreign Minister Shevardnadze at the White House on September 27. The discussions that Secretary Shultz and I had with the Foreign Minister were frank and useful. In my view they demonstrated that we both are working seriously on the problems which divide us as we near our meeting in Geneva. As I told Foreign Minister Shevardnadze, I look forward to the meeting and to the prospect of more constructive relations. I am considering carefully the arms control proposals contained in your letter and will be in touch with you on these questions in the near future.

This week I will address the UN General Assembly at the commemoration of the Fortieth Anniversary of the establishment of the United Nations. This anniversary is a valuable opportunity to reflect on the importance of the UN to world peace and security, as well as its unrealized potential. I think we both agree that the UN can and must be more effective in dealing with regional conflicts. In this connection, I noted Foreign Minister Shevardnadze's statement to the United Nations General Assembly that the Soviet Union viewed with alarm the fact that "it has not been possible to settle a single regional conflict or to extinguish a single hotbed of military tension."

We both recognize that the UN cannot by itself prevent such conflicts. All nations, particularly those directly involved, must devote their best efforts to reducing tensions and pursuing negotiated solutions to the most dangerous regional conflicts. Certainly our two nations have a major responsibility to encourage such efforts.

As I told Foreign Minister Shevardnadze, we have found our regional experts' discussions useful and propose to hold them on a regular basis. It is also desirable to try to build on this start by moving beyond the clarification of viewpoints to the search for concrete solutions to real problems. I hope that you and I can discuss this larger question in detail when we meet at Geneva. Even before then, however, I will put before the UN General Assembly an initiative to deal with an important groups of conflicts in Asia, Africa and Central America. I want you to be aware in advance of the proposal I will make.

Through our regional exchanges we have made clear our views on the nature of these problems and their impact on our overall relationship. Although our views on many aspects of these problems vary greatly, we believe that these disputes require political, not military, solutions, and we are prepared, if the Soviet Union is willing, to seek ways to help resolve conflicts through negotiation.

Because I believe in promoting a search for political solutions, I propose that we concentrate our efforts on those conflicts that did most to erode our relationship in the past. This would include Afghanistan, Cambodia, Nicaragua, Angola and Ethiopia. Of course, each of these conflicts has its own character and requirements, and we approach them with this fact in mind; other conflicts will need separate treatment altogether.

The peace program that I will put before the General Assembly seeks progress at three levels: internal reconciliation, superpower restraint, and economic reconstruction.

Because these conflicts are rooted in local disputes and problems, the starting point must be negotiations between the warring parties in each conflict; in the case of Afghanistan, this would obviously mean your own government. These talks may take different forms, but we believe that, together with improvement of internal political conditions, they are essential to achieving an end to violence, the withdrawal of foreign troops, and national reconciliation.

Once the parties to the conflicts make real progress, a second level of the process would be useful: separate U.S.-Soviet discussions, aimed at supporting the negotiating process between the warring parties. These talks would not be formal peace negotiations; needless to say, it is not for us to impose solutions. In some cases, however, it would be appropriate to consider guarantees for agreements reached. In every case the primary U.S.-Soviet role would be to support regional efforts to reduce and eliminate outside military involvement, including withdrawal of foreign troops and restraint on the flow of outside arms.

If the first two stages are successful, a third would then become possible: the reintegration of these countries into the world economy. The United States is prepared to contribute generously at this stage.

Foreign Minister Shevardnadze noted in his remarks at the United Nations General Assembly that in many cases mechanisms for mediation were already in place. We want to strengthen these existing mechanisms, and believe that this proposal will complement and reinforce them.

I feel that if we are unable to resolve these problems through negotiation among the real parties and through mutual restraint, they will only grow more difficult to resolve. This could lead to increased tensions – a situation that neither of us should welcome. I hope the Soviet Union is prepared to work constructively to help promote solutions to these conflicts, and will offer early support for my proposal. If so, you will find us willing to do our part, and to make the most of opportunities thereby opened for progress on other critical issues.

Sincerely,
Ronald Reagan

October 31, 1985

Dear Mr. General Secretary,

As I told Foreign Minister Shevardnadze in New York October 24, I have been giving careful consideration to your letter dated September 12. The issues you raise are important ones, the ideas you have put forward are in many ways interesting, and I have wanted to study them thoroughly before replying.

Many of the specific points you addressed in your letter have been or will be dealt with by our delegations in the Geneva arms control negotiations or by our Foreign Ministers. In this letter I will therefore focus on what I consider the most significant issues you have raised.

You suggested in your letter that we might reach an understanding on the inadmissibility of nuclear war and other general principles which should guide us. Foreign Minister Shevardnadze has since proposed specific language for our consideration. As I have repeatedly made clear, it is indeed my view that a nuclear war cannot be won and must never be fought. I therefore have instructed Secretary Shultz to discuss this matter with Foreign Minister Shevardnadze in their meetings next week.

As we address this and other elements which may figure in any document we may issue in Geneva, I believe it is important to give the most careful consideration to our words. The experience of the past has been that overly vague or rhetorical language has led to expectations which, given the competitive aspect of our relationship to which you referred in your letter, cannot be sustained.

If we are to avoid subsequent misunderstandings and disillusionment, our own statements should be clear and based on concrete achievements. I am convinced that there is substantial common ground on the range of areas we have been discussing in connection with our forthcoming meeting, and I would hope that this common ground can be expanded during our meeting in Geneva.

You raised several specific areas in the security field where this might be possible. Secretary Shultz will be prepared to discuss all your ideas in concrete terms while he is in Moscow. I believe you will find that we are indeed prepared to go our fair share of the way to ensure our meeting is a productive one.

I do, however, want to address your response to the proposals we had previously make in the Geneva arms control talks, which was foreshadowed in your letter and which your delegation subsequently tabled in Geneva.

We have been carefully assessing your counterproposal over the last month. As I stated in my address to the United Nations on October 24, I believe that within it there are seeds which we should nurture and that in the coming weeks we should seek to establish a genuine process of give-and-take.

In order to foster such a process, I have approved a new and comprehensive proposal designed to build upon the positive elements of your counterproposal and bridge the positions of our two sides. I have asked our negotiators to extend the current round to permit your experts to achieve a full understanding of our approach. This new proposal deals with all three areas under discussion in the Geneva negotiations. Its essence is a proposal for radical and stabilizing reductions in strategic offensive arms and a separate agreement on intermediate-range nuclear missile systems, both of which bridge US and Soviet ideas. We also propose that both sides provide assurances that their strategic defense programs are and will remain in full accord with the ABM Treaty. Such assurances assume a resolution of our current differences over compliance with the Treaty.

In the area of strategic arms, the United States agrees with the objective of a fifty percent reduction in strategic offensive forces. Our proposal builds on this, applying the fifty percent principle in a manner that is both equitable and can enhance stability. In the area of intermediate-range nuclear forces, we have also looked for elements we find in common. While I continue to firmly believe that the best outcome would be the complete elimination of intermediate-range nuclear missiles on both sides, in our new proposal, we have also moved in your direction. In defense and space we must begin now to establish a framework for a cooperative transition to more reliance on defenses and we would like to see more developed dialogue on how such a situation could be jointly undertaken.

We have designed our approach to provide for a mutually acceptable resolution of the range of nuclear and space arms issues; to take account of the interrelationship between the offense and the defense; and to address those concerns that you and your negotiators have described as being of great importance to you. I am convinced that this new proposal can provide the basis for immediate and genuine progress on the numerous and complex issues facing us in the nuclear and space area, and I look forward to discussing it with you in Geneva later this month.

We will also have the opportunity in Geneva to discuss the other areas which make up our relationship. Much work remains to be done if we are to be able to announce specific progress on regional and bilateral issues. I hope that Secretary Shultz's Moscow visit will be a stimulus to rapid progress in the weeks ahead.

In conclusion, may I say once more that I am looking forward to our meeting and that I sincerely hope we will be able to set our countries on a *less confrontational and more cooperative course in the years ahead. I will personally spare no effort to help bring this about.*

Sincerely,

Ronald Reagan

November 1, 1985

Dear Mr. General Secretary,

This is in reply to your letter of October 12, 1985, concerning the possibility of a confidential exchange of opinions on a non-official basis. My reasons for mentioning this possibility to Foreign Minister Shevardnadze were twofold.

First, it seemed there could be some intrinsic value in exchanging opinions informally and privately without the constraints imposed by official formality. But I also wished to resolve certain ambiguities in how we communicate. From time to time in recent months Soviet officials have approached American officials or private citizens who are in touch with senior officials in our government and have offered comments which, they suggest, represent your views. Naturally, I have paid close attention to these comments since I take your opinions very seriously and wish to do the utmost to understand them with full clarity. However, the comments received in this manner have not always been consistent and thus I have difficulty determining to what degree they in fact represent your views. It therefore seemed worthwhile to seek a clarification.

I judge from your reply that you consider established channels adequate for communication between us. That is agreeable to me. Consequently Secretary Shultz will continue to look forward to receiving Ambassador Dobrynin at the State Department. Similarly, we will expect that Ambassador Hartman will enjoy corresponding access to you in Moscow.

I hope that the meetings Secretary Shultz has in Moscow will lay the groundwork for a productive meeting between us in Geneva. I am very much looking forward to meeting you there and continue to hope that we will succeed in setting relations between our two countries on a more constructive course.

Sincerely,

Ronald Reagan

THE GENEVA SUMMIT
NOVEMBER 21-22, 1985

When President Reagan and General Secretary Gorbachev met in Geneva, Switzerland, it was the first meeting in seven years between the leaders of the United States and the Soviet Union. Tensions were naturally high, fueled by the hundreds of international television and newspaper reporters covering the Summit.

Reagan and Gorbachev decided to open the Summit with a private meeting. Only interpreters and note-takers were invited. Reagan characterized U.S.-Soviet relations as "peaceful competition". Gorbachev emphasized "cooperation rather than confrontation" and the importance of halting the arms race. Both agreed that distrust would be the main obstacle to any agreements. "In the meeting with the larger group, where we should soon move," Reagan told Gorbachev, "the sides can explain why there is mistrust, but can also begin to try to eliminate this mistrust." Gorbachev agreed.

In the first plenary session later that day, Gorbachev welcomed Reagan's proposal for further exchanges in the areas of science and technology because the exchanges would help remove the distrust that currently exists between the two nations. Reagan took that as his cue to try and convince Gorbachev that SDI research would only be for defensive purposes. To emphasize his point Reagan called SDI a "shield". The president also criticized Gorbachev for trying to curtail American SDI research and development claiming that the Soviet Union was also conducting "the same kind of research program." "If one or both of us come up with such a system," Reagan added, "then they should sit down and make it available to everyone so no one would have a fear of a nuclear strike." Gorbachev held his response until the afternoon session.

"We think SDI can lead to an arms race in space, and not just a defensive arms race, but an offensive arms race with space weapons," Gorbachev told Reagan after lunch. The General Secretary continued,

Space weapons are harder to verify and will feed suspicions and mistrust. Scientists say any shield can be pierced, so SDI cannot save us. So why create it? It only makes sense if to defend against a retaliatory strike....

I know that you, Mr. President, are attached to SDI, and for that reason we have analyzed it seriously. Our conclusion is that if the U.S. implements its plan, we will not cooperate in an effort to gain superiority over us. We will have to frustrate this plan, and we will build up in order to smash your shield.

You say the Soviet Union is doing the same, but this is not the case. Both of us do research in space of course, but our research is for peaceful purposes. The U.S., in contrast has military aims, and that is an important difference. The U.S. goal violates the ABM Treaty, which is of fundamental importance. Testing is also inconsistent with the Treaty, and can only exacerbate mistrust.

If the U.S. embarks on SDI the following will happen: (1) No reduction of offensive weapons; and (2) We will respond. This response will not be a mirror image of your program, but a simpler, more effective system.

Three more private meetings and two plenary sessions followed over the next two days, but both Reagan and Gorbachev were committed to their positions. All was not lost, however, because Gorbachev agreed to visit Washington, and Reagan agreed to visit Moscow. Most importantly, Reagan and Gorbachev agreed to separate talks on intermediate range nuclear weapons and space weapons so that intermediate range nuclear forces "would not be held hostage to progress in space talks." NATO countries must have also been pleased when Reagan reported to them after the Summit that the Soviet Union agreed to reduce their intermediate range forces capable of striking targets in Europe to the same level of NATO forces at the end of the year.

CHAPTER TWO

Preparing for Reykjavik

November 28, 1985
Letter from Reagan to Gorbachev
(See endnotes for transcription)

THE WHITE HOUSE
WASHINGTON

Nov. 28 '85

Dear Secretary General Gorbachev

Now that we are both home & facing the task of leading our countries into a more constructive relationship with each other, I wanted to waste no time in giving you some of my initial thoughts on our meetings. Though I will be sending shortly, in a more formal & official manner, a more detailed commentary on our discussions, there are some things I would like to convey very personally & privately.

First, I want you to know that I found our meetings of great value. We had agreed to speak frankly, and we did. As a result, I came away from the meeting with a better understanding of your attitudes. I hope you also understand mine a little better. Obviously there are many things on which we disagree and disagree very fundamentally. But if I understand you correctly, you too are determined to take steps to see that our nations manage their relations in a peaceful fashion. If this is the case, then this is one point on which we are in total agreement — and it is after all the most fundamental one of all.

THE WHITE HOUSE

WASHINGTON

As for our substantive differences, let me offer some thoughts on two of the key ones.

Regarding strategic defense and it's relation to the reduction of offensive nuclear weapons, I was struck by your conviction that the American program is somehow designed to secure a strategic advantage -- even to permit a first strike capability. I also noted your concern that research & testing in this area could be a cover for developing & placing offensive weapons in space.

As I told you, neither of these concerns is warranted. But I can understand, as you explained so eloquently, that these are matters which cannot be taken on faith. Both of us must cope with what the other side is doing, & judge the implications for the security of his own country. I do not ask you to take my assurances on faith.

However the truth is that the United States has no intention of using it's strategic defense program to gain any advantage, & there is no development underway to create space-based offensive weapons. Our goal is to eliminate any possibility of a first strike from either side. This being the case, we should be able to find a way, in practical terms,

THE WHITE HOUSE

WASHINGTON

to relieve the concerns you have expressed.

For example, could our negotiators, when they resume work in January, discuss frankly & specifically what sort of future developments each of us would find threatening? Neither of us, it seems, wants to see offensive weapons, particularly weapons of mass destruction, deployed in space. Should we not attempt to define what sort of systems have that potential and then try to find verifiable ways to prevent their development?

And can't our negotiators deal more frankly & openly with the question of how to eliminate a first-strike potential on both sides? Your military now has an advantage in this area — a three to one advantage in warheads that can destroy hardened targets with little warning. That is obviously alarming to us, & explains many of the efforts we are making in our modernization program. You may feel perhaps that the U.S. has some advantage in other categories. If so, let's insist that our negotiators face up to these issues & find a way to improve the security of both countries by agreeing on appropriately balanced reductions. If you are as sincere as I am in not seeking to secure or preserve one-sided advantages, we will find a solution to these problems.

THE WHITE HOUSE

WASHINGTON

Regarding another key issue we discussed, that of regional conflicts, I can assure you that the United States does not believe that the Soviet Union is the cause of all the world's ills. We do believe, however, that your country has exploited and worsened local tensions & conflict by militarizing them and, indeed, intervening directly & indirectly in struggles arising out of local causes. While we both will doubtless continue to support our friends, we must find a way to do so without use of armed force. This is the crux of the point I tried to make.

One of the most significant steps in lowering tension in the world — & tension in U. S.-Soviet relations — would be a decision on your part to withdraw your forces from Afghanistan. I gave careful attention to your comments on this issue at Geneva, and am encouraged by your statement that you feel political reconciliation is possible. I want you to know that I am prepared to cooperate in any reasonable way to facilitate such a withdrawal, & that I understand that it must be done in a manner which does not damage Soviet security interests. During our meetings I mentioned one idea which I thought might be helpful & I will welcome any further suggestions you may have.

THE WHITE HOUSE
WASHINGTON

These are only two of the key issues on our current agenda. I will soon send some thoughts on others. I believe that we should act promptly to build the momentum our meeting initiated.

In Geneva I found our private sessions particularly useful. Both of us have advisors & assistants, but, you know, in the final analysis, the responsibility to preserve peace & increase cooperation is ours. Our people look to us for leadership, and nobody can provide it if we don't. But we won't be very effective leaders unless we can rise above the specific but secondary concerns that preoccupy our respective bureaucracies & give our governments a strong push in the right direction.

So, what I want to say finally is that we should make the most of the time before we meet again to find some specific & significant steps that would give meaning to our commitment to peace & arms reduction. Why not set a goal — privately, first between the two of us — to find a practical way to solve critical issues — the two I have mentioned — by the time we meet in Washington?

Please convey regards from Nancy & me to Mrs. Gorbacheva. We genuinely enjoyed meeting you in Geneva & are already looking forward to showing you something of our country next year.

Sincerely yours, Ronald Reagan

[Unlike Reagan's November 28 letter, which focused on strategic defense and a Soviet withdrawal from Afghanistan, Gorbachev used his first letter after the Geneva Summit to focus on a mutual agreement to ban nuclear testing. The Soviet Union, Gorbachev reminded Reagan, had already unilaterally imposed a moratorium on nuclear testing, but would be forced to resume testing in January if the United States did not also agree to a moratorium on nuclear testing.

Gorbachev also does not mention Reagan's letter of November 28. Perhaps the general secretary was still reflecting on how best to respond to Reagan's November 28 proposals, or more likely he had not yet received that letter before writing his December 5th letter. Whatever the case, Gorbachev's formal response to Reagan's November 28 proposals came a few weeks later, on December 24.]

December 5, 1985

Dear Mr. President,

In this message of mine I would like to express some considerations and proposals as a follow-up to our exchange of views.

After the Geneva meeting we have a common task – to do all that is necessary and possible so that its results which were met with satisfaction everywhere, be reinforced by practical agreements and measures leading to the termination of the arms race, strengthening of the security of all states and revitalization of the situation in the world. This is precisely what is expected of us as leaders of the two major powers.

The Soviet-American talks on nuclear and space weapons are, of course, of special importance. We favor achieving real progress at these talks, as well as at the conference in Stockholm, at the negotiations in Vienna and in other fora.

But there is an issue where concrete and rather weighty and tangible results can be achieved already now. This is the issue of stopping nuclear tests.

The Soviet Union unilaterally introduced since August 6 and has been observing a moratorium on all nuclear explosions. There is no need to dwell upon the seriousness of this step. To take such a decision was not a simple matter for us. The Soviet side has its own programs, concrete practical needs. For that reason a time periods through which the moratorium would remain in effect was set – until January 1, 1986. As we have stated, the USSR is ready to refrain from conducting nuclear explosions even further, though, naturally, on the basis of reciprocity. I wish to reaffirm that again. If, however, no positive response to this goodwill gesture of ours comes from the US, the unilateral commitments of the USSR will be void after the announced date.

We would not like it to happen. Although we do not have much time at our disposal, there is still enough time for the American side to carefully analyze this question again and to review it in broad political terms. I wish to reiterate the thought which I have already expressed to you: if there is a genuine intention to work towards stopping the nuclear arms race, a mutual moratorium cannot be objected to, while it would bring great benefits.

Indeed – what can be the objective obstacles to our joint suspension of nuclear weapon tests? I am convinced that there are no such obstacles. For in that case our countries would, in fact, be in an equal position.

Sometimes, of course, they refer to the difficulties of verification. But there is no basis whatsoever to dramatize this problem, either. We both know that the USSR and the US possess very sophisticated national technical means making it possible to verify reliably the fact of the absence of nuclear explosions. An additional guarantee of ensuring the confidence of the sides that the moratorium is being observed would be renouncing – as the Soviet Union has done now – any nuclear explosions – for peaceful, as well as military purposes.

If, however, some doubts regarding verification remain, this, given agreement on the main point, is a problem which, in our view, can be solved. One can take up, for example, the proposal of the Delhi "six" – Argentina, Greece, India, Mexico, Tanzania and Sweden – regarding the creation of verification mechanisms on the territories of these countries. We have already expressed a positive attitude to that.

Moreover, if a natural moratorium on nuclear explosions is going to be introduced now, we are prepared – and this is what we propose – to agree at the same time on the following: on a reciprocal basis to give on appropriate requests the opportunity to the observers of both sides to visit the locations of ambiguous phenomena in order to remove possible doubts that such phenomena can be related to nuclear explosions.

In other words, the issue of a mutual moratorium on nuclear explosions is ripe and can be resolved as a practical matter. And if one is to speak of the political significance of such a joint step, then, certainly, it would give quite a definite signal to other nuclear powers, too, would create a qualitatively new situation much more favorable for a positive development of the process started in Geneva, for taking effective practical steps to curb the nuclear arms race.

The resumption of the trilateral negotiations on the general and complete prohibition of nuclear weapon tests would also be a tangible step in that direction. The overwhelming majority of states quite definitely *speaks in favor of that, as was clearly stated in the U.N., at the recent NPT review conference, in other prestigious international organizations.*

I would like to reaffirm our readiness for such negotiations and I specifically propose that they be resumed next January, for example, in Geneva. I believe that, should you accept, we could jointly come to terms on this matter with the British, too.

Mr. President, I found it necessary to address in this message a very important, serious question in the spirit of frankness which permeated our meetings and conversations in Geneva.

On behalf of the Soviet leadership I would like to reaffirm that we favor the implementation of those understandings of principle, which were reached between us. It is precisely in this vein that I address you.

We do not seek any genuinely convincing reasons, why the USSR and the US could not make a joint step – to mutually discontinue nuclear explosions. A political decision is required in this case. And we would like to hope that such a decision will be taken by the US Administration.

Sincerely,

M. GORBACHEV

December 7, 1985

Dear Mr. General Secretary,

The visit of Secretary Baldrige to the USSR provides and excellent opportunity for me to give you confidentially some of my further thinking on the issue of human rights. I was encouraged by our discussions on this topic in Geneva. Neither of us, I am sure, expected to convince the other of the correctness of all our positions during those sessions. However, I was pleased by your apparent agreement that this is a subject on which, working quietly, we can resolve outstanding problems.

You noted your support for contacts between our two peoples, the importance of visits by relatives, and your understanding of the need for increased contacts by religious groups. You agreed that it is natural that our citizens should marry I Hope steps will be taken that eliminate artificial barriers in these and similar areas. We agreed that the time has come for boldness in our relationship. I can assure you that some bold steps in the human rights area would be reciprocated by us in other areas.

At Geneva, I noted our pleasure that our embassy had been informed that a number of separated spouses would be allowed to leave the Soviet Union to join their husbands or wives. Some unfortunately have yet to hear this officially. Moreover, we have difficulty reconciling your number of ten spouses being held for a limited time because of security concerns with the longer list of such people who we know seek to be united with their loved ones. One of these cases involves a blind Soviet woman in her sixties who had been separated from her husband for almost thirty years. Another longtime case involves a Soviet man driven by desperation into two life-threatening hunger strikes in an effort to join his wife and small children in the United States. Several other cases have remained unresolved for many years.

We have provided your government with a list of 17 names in addition to those we have already been informed will be released; they all deserve special concern, and their resolution would be a positive impact on the relationship. I fervently hope these cases can be resolved quickly. It would be a joyous occasion if all of them could join their spouses for the Christmas and New Year's holidays.

I also hope we can overcome whatever obstacles stand in the way of eliminating the problem of people with dual US-Soviet citizenship. There are 23 of these cases. Several of these people are now very old. One 77-year old U.S. citizen, who came to the Soviet Union in 1932 on a school break and somehow ended up with a Soviet internal passport, has been trying unsuccessfully to return to the United States for over 50 years. None of the people involved raise security issues in any way whatsoever; it should be easy to wipe the slate clean in this area by allowing those who wish to depart to do so – quickly.

There are an additional one-hundred twenty-nine families in the Soviet Union who want to join close relatives in the United States, but have not been allowed to do so. Each one of these cases involves a human tragedy of separation. One involves a 16-year old child from Leningrad whose father was killed in an automobile accident last fall, leaving him all alone. In many other cases, parents and children have been separated for many years. Our embassy has in the past and will again provide all necessary details on these cases.

Beyond these cases, let me touch on areas in which, as I mentioned in Geneva, there are quite substantial political incentives for progress. I refer here to the broad question of emigration, whether of members of such groups as Jews, Armenians, and others, or of some internationally-known individuals. In both categories, we are talking about quite poignant cases. The young pianist I mentioned to you falls into the category of someone whose requests to emigrate have been refused. The political importance of resolving such well known cases as the Sakharov's, Anatoliy Shcharanskiy, and Yuri Orlov cannot be overestimated. We are not interested in exploiting these cases. Their resolution will permit greater prominence for other issues in relationship.

I mentioned the need for boldness in dealing with these issues. We are prepared to take some bold steps ourselves in areas that Secretary Baldrige will be willing to discuss. The emigration and trade areas offer some real scope for parallel movement that could benefit both our countries. I hope you and your representatives will discuss these areas candidly with Secretary Baldrige.

I trust that after our discussions in Geneva you have no doubt about my desire to move the relationship between our two countries onto a more constructive path. The issues I have laid out in this letter are serious ones. Progress here would provide an enormous impetus to the resolution of other outstanding problems; lack of progress will only us back.

Sincerely,
Ronald Reagan

[General Secretary Gorbachev seemed to have been particularly affected by President Reagan's November 28, 1985 letter. Perhaps it was that Reagan handwrote the letter, but more likely it was the informal nature and friendly tone. "I attach special significance to the fact that we have been able to overcome the serious psychological barrier which for a long time has hindered a dialogue worthy of the leaders of the USSR and the USA," Gorbachev noted. Gorbachev responded in kind.

Despite the mutual shift in tone, Gorbachev could not have been more clear in his response to Reagan's November 28 proposals. In terms of SDI, Gorbachev reiterated that the Soviet Union would respond with their own system if the United States continued to develop space-based weapons capable of traveling thousands of miles and destroying Soviet targets within minutes. In terms of regional conflicts, Gorbachev told Reagan that American support for "terrorists" in Afghanistan and Nicaragua made the situation worse, and that the Soviet Union was only involved in those countries at the request of their democratically elected government.]

December 24, 1985

Dear Mr. President:

I consider your letter important and also value the form you used in writing to me.

I say this to you because I see the desire to continue and to strengthen what we achieved in Geneva. I am glad that we began there – both in substance and in spirit – a direct and frank discussion. I attach special significance to the fact that we have been able to overcome the serious psychological barrier which for a long time has hindered a dialogue worthy of the leaders of the USSR and the USA.

I have the feeling that now you and I can set formalities aside and can get down to the heart of the matter – establishing a specific topical agenda for the discussion over the next few years on the basis of our understanding, and straightening out Soviet-American relations. I visualize this task very concretely: we have to broaden areas of agreement, strengthen the elements of responsibleness in our policy, and make the appropriate practical decisions. In my opinion the ideal situation would be one in which you and I would give impetus to a constant forward movement. I agree with what you said: in the final analysis no one besides us can do this.

The first thing we should do is to take upon ourselves the task of undoing the knot which has been tied around the issues of nuclear and space weapons. I was encouraged by the fact that you, Mr. President, also consider that this is of key significance.

I think you understood from what I told you in Geneva that our decisive opposition to the development of space-strike weapons is dictated by the fact that weapons of this class which, due to their specific nature, possess the capability of being used both for defensive and offensive aims, represent in the final analysis an extremely dangerous build-up of offensive potential, with all the consequences inevitably ensuing therefrom from the point of view of further escalating the arms race.

You say, Mr. President, that the U.S. has no intention of using the SDI program to obtain military superiority.

I do not doubt that you personally may really have no such intentions. But you must agree that the leadership of one side has to evaluate the actions of the other in the area of developing new types of weapons, not in accordance with intentions, but in accordance with the potential capabilities which may be attained as a result of the development of these weapons.

Examining the SDI program from this perceptive, the Soviet leadership comes to the same conclusion every time: given the realities of the current situation, only a country which is preparing for a first (disarming) strike needs a "space shield"; a country which does not base its actions on such a concept should have no need for such a weapons system.

After all, space-strike weapons are all-purpose weapons. The space-strike weapons that are being created in the U.S. are kinetic energy weapons and also long-range, directed energy systems (with a range of several thousand miles and great destructive power). As our experts and scientists and yours confirm, those weapons are capable of destroying in space, as well as from space, within a very short time, in great quantities and selectively, objects which are thousands of miles away. I stress – thousands of miles away.

For example, how should we regard the space weapons of a country which have the capability of destroying another country's centers for a controlling space objects and of destroying its space devices for monitoring, navigation, communication etc. within very short time intervals measured in minutes? Essentially, these weapons can only be intended for "blinding" the other side, catching it unprepared and depriving it of the possibility of countering a nuclear strike. Moreover, if these weapons are developed, the process of perfecting them and giving them even better combat characteristics will begin immediately. Such is the course of development of all weaponry.

Now then, Mr. President, should the Soviet Union act in such a situation? I would like to repeat what I already told you in Geneva. The USSR cannot simply reduce and will not reduce nuclear weapons to the detriment of its security, when the SDI program is being implemented in the U.S. Whether we like it or not we will be forced to develop and improve our strategic nuclear forces and increase their capability of neutralizing the U.S. "space shield." At the same time, we would also have to develop our own space weapons inter alia for the purpose of a territorial ABM defense. Probably, the U.S. would in turn then take some other additional steps. As a result, we will not get out of the vicious cycle of measures and countermeasures, out of the whirlpool of an ever-increasing arms race. The consequence of such competition for our peoples and for all of mankind is unpredictable.

I am convinced that the only sensible way out is not to engage in this at all. From every point of view the correct path for our countries is negotiation on the prevention of an arms race in space and its cessation on earth. And we need to come to agreement on the basis of equal and mutually acceptable conditions.

You and I agreed to accelerate the negotiations. I took satisfaction in hearing you say that the U.S. would not "develop space-based offensive weapons."

As I see it, some kind of common basis is emerging between you and me for a very significant part of the problem of preventing an arms race in space. Let us have our representatives at the negotiations proceed on this basis to begin working out specific measures to prevent the development of offensive space weapons, i.e., all space-based weapons which can destroy targets in space and from space.

In the spirit of the frankness in which we are talking, I would like to say that this issue has now become very acute: either events will determine policy or we will determine policy. In order not to be governed by events, it *is especially important once again to conduct a profound analysis of all aspects of the objective interrelationship between offensive and defensive weapons and to hear such other out on this issue. However, it seems to me that there will be little meaning to such discussions if in tandem with them weapons of war start coming out the doors of our laboratories, weapons whose influence on strategic stability we must not now miscalculate. Common sense dictates that until we determine together those consequences, we must not permit anything to go beyond the walls of the laboratory. We are prepared to negotiate to reach agreement on this matter as well.*

It appears to me this is a practical way to implement the joint accord you and I confirmed in Geneva concerning the inadmissibility of an arms race in space and concerning the ultimate elimination of nuclear arms.

In line with such an approach it would also make sense at the Geneva negotiations to discuss the issue of eliminating the danger of first (disarming) nuclear strike. I would like to state to you again very definitely: we are not making a bid for a first nuclear strike, we are not preparing our nuclear force for one.

I cannot agree with the way you formulate the issue of first strike nuclear forces. This issue, of course, is not merely one of ICBM warheads. For example, there is no difference between U.S. ballistic missile warheads on "Trident" submarines and warheads on modern Soviet land-based intercontinental ballistic missiles as far as their kill capability is concerned, i.e. in terms of such indices as accuracy, power and range. And if one considers this issue from the point of view of warning time, then, for a significant portion of submarine missiles, where the U.S. has a three-fold advantage in warheads, the warning time is significantly shorter.

And can we view the "Pershing II" missiles deployed in Europe with their high accuracy and short flight time to targets on USSR territory as anything other than first-strike weapons?

Please forgive me for dealing with technical details in a personal letter like this. But there are vitally important realities, and we simply cannot get around them.

Believe me, Mr. President, we have a genuine and truly serious concern about U.S. nuclear systems. You talk about mutual concerns. This matter can be resolved only through considering and counting the sum total of the respective nuclear systems of both countries. Let our delegations discuss this matter as well.

Mr. President, I would like to give you my brief reaction to what you said concerning regional conflicts. At the time when we touched on these issues in Geneva, I stressed that it is most important to view things realistically, to see the world as it is. If we recognize the fact that independent states exist and function in the international arena, then we also have to acknowledge their sovereign right to have relations with whomever they wish and the right to ask for assistance, including military assistance.

Both you and we offer such assistance. Why apply a double standard and assert that Soviet assistance is a source of tension and U.S. assistance is beneficial? It would be better for us to be guided by objective criteria in this matter. The Soviet Union is assisting legitimate governments which come to us because they have been and are being subjected to outside military interference.

And, as the facts indicate, the U.S. incites actions against governments and supports and supplies weapons to groups which are inimical to society and which are, in essence, terrorists. Looking at things objectively, it is such actions and outside interference that create regional tension and conflict. If such actions cease, I am convinced tensions will decrease and the prospects for political settlements will become much better and more realistic.

Unfortunately, at present, developments are proceeding in a different direction. Take, for example, the unprecedented pressure and threats which the government of Nicaragua is being subjected to – a legitimate government brought to power through free elections.

I will be frank: what the United States has done recently causes concern. It seems that there is a tilt in the direction of further exacerbation of regional problems. Such an approach does not make it easier to find a common language and makes the search for political solutions more difficult.

With regard to Afghanistan, one gets the impression that the U.S. side intentionally fails to notice the "open door" leading to a political settlement. Now there is even a working formula for such a settlement. It is important not to hinder the negotiations in progress, but to help them along. In that event a fair settlement will definitely be found.

Mr. President, I would like to have you take my letter as another of our "fireside talks." I would truly like to preserve not only the spirit of our Geneva meetings, but also to go further in developing our dialogue. I view our correspondence as a very important channel for preparing for our meeting in Washington.

The new year will be upon us very soon, and I would like to send you and your wife our very best wishes.

Sincerely,
M. Gorbachev

["The fact that the President wrote the letter in longhand obviously made an impression," the Department of State analysis of Gorbachev's letter started. "Gorbachev not only answered in kind, but with an unusual lack of formality." The State analysis continued,

> Gorbachev, however, is characteristically unyielding on substance, whether arms control or regional issues. On the former, he basically reaffirms current Soviet positions, dwelling, as in Geneva, on SDI.
>
> Gorbachev's extensive treatment of SDI is most interesting for his suggestion that the President's earlier assurances that the U.S. will not develop 'offensive space-based weapons' might serve as 'common ground' for discussion in Geneva. His definition of such weapons – all space-based weapons capable of destroying targets in space or from space – would have the practical effect of barring many potentially promising SDI technologies. But his expression of willingness to discuss the offense-defense relationship in detail appears to take the Soviet position beyond its previous refusal of U.S. proposals for a serious dialogue in this area.]

December 26, 1985

Dear Mr. General Secretary:

I have already written to you informally to express some of my thoughts on the issues facing us in the wake of our meeting in Geneva. I would like in this letter to deal with some of the particularly pressing regional issues which I believe we must address in the months ahead.

I mentioned Afghanistan in my earlier letter, but I would like to share with you some further thoughts. Afghanistan was, after all, the regional question on which we spent the most time in Geneva. You expressed Soviet readiness to see an agreement emerge from the United Nations negotiating process which would entail a ceasefire, withdrawal of troops, return of the refugees and international guarantees. The discussion recalled the suggestion in your June 10 letter that my government had "opportunities to confirm by its actions" our readiness to reach a political settlement in Afghanistan. As I explained in my October speech to the UNGA, we are prepared to cooperate with others on practical steps. Three elements could form the basis for a lasting solution: A process of negotiations among the warring parties including the Soviet Union; verified elimination of the foreign military presence and restraint on the flow of outside arms; and movement toward political self-determination and economic reconstruction.

As you know, we have been disappointed with the results of the proximity talks conducted by the U.N. Secretary General's Special Representative. Five rounds in Geneva have not addressed the real issue on which a resolution of this problem depends – withdrawal of your forces. No other element of the problem presents real difficulty.

To understand this, we have formally notified the Secretary General that we accept the agreed formulation on guarantees. For your part, I believe that the talks would gain a real impetus from Soviet action to permit discussion of a timetable for withdrawal at Geneva and a public announcement to that effect. Were such action taken by the time of our Ministers' next meeting, it would enable them to have a more focused and productive discussion.

Another area where I believe movement is possible is Southern Africa. Because we have covered this ground often in the past, the point I need to make is a simple one.

As I am sure you are aware, I am reviewing our policy in Southern Africa, specifically with respect to the war in Angola. This review might not be necessary if there were real evidence that the outside forces in that country could be reduced, and then withdrawn, making possible the reconciliation of the indigenous parties to the war. Such an outcome, of course, would dramatically improve prospects for the establishment of an independent Namibia in accordance with UNSC Resolution 435 – an objective we share with the U.S.S.R. Unfortunately, the evidence is clear that your own involvement in Angola is deepening.

As I said at the UN in October, our aim is to reduce, not increase, military involvement by the superpowers in local disputes like that in Angola.

I was pleased to learn from Secretary Shultz that the Soviet Union had expressed an interest in calming tensions between Libya and Egypt. At the same time, it appears that Libya is preparing at least two sites for the emplacement of SA-5 Air Defense Missiles to be supplied by the Soviet Union. It is hard to reconcile Soviet interest in restraint in this region with the provision of advanced weapons to a leader whose reckless behavior is a major danger to regional stability. Because we view this development with utmost seriousness, I was disappointed to see that the Soviet response to our presentation failed to address the transfer of these weapons to Libya. Our Ministers and experts should address this vital matter, since it raises the prospect of dangerous incidents that I hope you want to avoid as much as we do.

If you agree, both Angola and Libya are additional subjects which Secretary Shultz and Foreign Minister Shevardnadze might take up in their next meeting.

In closing, let me underline my satisfaction with our agreement in Geneva to put our regional experts' talks on a regular basis. When we met in Geneva we agreed that it was important for both of us to avoid a U.S.-Soviet clash over regional conflicts and to work for solutions. I believe that we must move forward on some of these issues before we meet again. In that regard, I was pleased to note that in your remarks to Secretary Baldrige you referred to the importance of dealing with regional trouble spots.

Sincerely,
Ronald Reagan

January 11, 1986

Dear Mr. President,

Your letter of December 7, transmitted through Secretary Baldrige, addressed the questions on which we had a rather thorough discussion in Geneva. At that time I outlined in detail our approach to these questions, and, it seemed to me, you took in what was said with certain understanding.

It is hardly necessary to repeat, that the questions involved pertain to the internal competence of our state and that they are resolved in strict conformity with the laws. I would like only to point out, that the Soviet laws do not create impediments when decisions are taken on the questions regarding departures from the USSR by Soviet citizens who have legal grounds for that. This is attested to also by the fact that as a practical matter the overwhelming majority of such questions is resolved positively.

The existing laws are obligatory to everybody – both to those who apply to leave and those who consider exist applications. Such is the essence of our law and order and nobody is entitled to violate it – whether under any pressure or without it. I would think this should be understood in the U.S.

We, of course, take into account, that due to various circumstances, divided families appear, which live partially in the USSR and partially – in the USA. Only in the past 5 years there have been over 400 marriages between Soviet and American citizens. And the overwhelming majority of those marriages – to be precise, more than 95 percent – encountered no problems with regard to the reunification of the spouse and to living together. Yes, there are exceptions, and we have frankly and repeatedly told you what they are about. But generally, and I want to stress it again, questions of this kinds are resolved by us on the basis of humanism and taking into account the interests of the people concerned.

I share your desire to channel the relationship between our countries to a more constructive course. And the breaks are being put on this process in no way due to the existence of the cases of such sort – though I do not tend to belittle their importance from the point of view of the lives of individual persons – but because of the attempts to blow them out of proportion in the general balance of Soviet-American relations. The key issues in this area are awaiting their resolution.

I would like to note in passing: as it can be seen, the continued attempts by the American side to tie up trade and economic relations with questions of a different nature will bring no benefit. It is high time to take a realistic look at this whole issue from the position of today, rather than yesterday.

It would seem that much will now depend on how accurately we are going to follow jointly the real priorities in our relations, if we wish to bring about their tangible normalization already in the near future. I think, the chances are not bad here.

Sincerely,

M. GORBACHEV

[Reagan's formal response to Gorbachev's December 24 letter, dated February 16, was handwritten at the suggestion of Ambassador Matlock, who was at the time the soviet specialist on the National Security Council.

Significantly, the tone of Reagan's letter was more positive than past letters. Reagan talked about "immediate progress", and noted that disagreements on a chemical weapons ban and reducing intermediate range ballistic missiles "seem to be falling away."

But significant disagreements over SDI still lingered. Reagan, this time, tried to turn Gorbachev's arguments against him by claiming that the United States should be fearful of Soviet research and development in the area of space attack weapons because the Soviet Union was the only country to have a working anti-ballistic missile system that had been tested to strike targets in space. Specifically addressing Gorbachev's concern that SDI was a cover for placing nuclear weapons in space, Reagan also said he was optimistic that they could work out a verification process to alleviate the general secretary's concerns. Again, he promised that the United States had no intentions of placing offensive weapons in space.

In terms of significant arms reductions, Reagan reiterated his agreement that they should continue to work towards a 50 percent reduction in nuclear weapons. But, Reagan wrote, he still needed more time to formulate an appropriate response to Gorbachev's call for the complete elimination of nuclear weapons by the year 2000.

Reagan also devoted time in this letter to regional issues. The president repeated that he saw no basis for the Soviet invasion of Afghanistan and again called for a total withdrawal of Soviet troops. He informed Gorbachev that if he immediately pulled all the Soviet troops our of Afghanistan U.S.-Soviet relations would also dramatically improve.]

February 16, 1986

Dear Mr. General Secretary,

Your letter of Dec. 24, 1985 was most thought provoking and I would like to share my reactions with you. I have of course also received your letter of Jan. 14, 1986, and will be responding to it shortly.[11] However, since the substance of the letter is already in the public domain, I believe it is well to keep our private communications separate. Although the issues overlap, I would hope that our informal exchange can be used to clarify our attitudes on some of the fundamental questions.

I agree with you that we need to set a specific agenda for action to bring about a steady – and I would hope – radical improvement in U.S.-Soviet relations. I suggested two such topics in my previous letter, and I would hope that we can identify others as ripe for immediate progress. For example, some of the obstacles to an agreement on intermediate-range missiles seem to be falling away. I would also hope that rapid progress can be made toward agreement on a verification regime that will permit a global ban on chemical weapons.

Regarding arms reduction in general, I agree with you that we must make decisions not on the basis of assurances or intentions but with regard to the capabilities on both sides. Nevertheless, I do not understand the reasoning behind your conclusion that only a country preparing a disarming first strike would be interested in defenses against ballistic missiles. If such defense prove possible in the future, they could facilitate further reductions of nuclear weapons by creating a feeling of confidence that national security could be preserved without them.

Of course, as I have said before, I recognize that adding defensive systems to an arsenal replete with weapons with a disarming first-strike capability could under some conditions be destabilizing. That is why we are

---

[11] Gorbachev's January 14, 1986 letter could not be located. According to the public statements, Gorbachev's letter outlined his proposal for the complete elimination of nuclear weapons by the year 2000.

proposing that both sides concentrate first on reducing those weapons which can be used to deliver a disarming first strike. Certainly, if neither of our countries has forces suitable for a first strike, neither need fear that defense against ballistic missiles would make a first strike strategy possible.

I also do not understand your statement that what you call "space strike weapons" are "all purpose" weapons. As I understand it, the sort of directed-energy and kinetic devise both our countries are investigating in the context of ballistic missile defense are potentially most effective against point targets moving at high velocity in space. They would be ill-suited for mass destruction on earth, and if one were planning to strike earth targets from space, it does not seem rational to resort to such expensive and exotic techniques. Their destructiveness can never approach that of the nuclear weapons in our hands today. Nuclear weapons are the real problem.

Mr. General Secretary, in the spirit of candor which is essential to effective communication, I would add another point. You spoke often of "space strike weapons", and your representatives have defined these as weapons which can strike targets in space from earth and its atmosphere, and weapons in space which can strike targets in space or on earth. I must ask, "What country has such weapons?" The answer is only one: the Soviet Union. Your ABM system deployed around Moscow can strike targets beyond the atmosphere and has been tested in that mode. Your co-orbital anti-satellite weapon is designed to destroy satellites. Furthermore, the Soviet Union began research in defenses utilizing directed energy before the United States did and seems well along in research (and – incidentally – some testing outside laboratories) of lasers and other forms of directed energy.

I do not point this out in reproach or suggest that these activities are in violation of agreements. But if we were to follow your logic to the effect that what you call "space strike weapons" would only be developed by a country planning a first strike, what would we think? We see the Soviet Union devoting enormous resources to defensive systems in an effort which antedates by many years our own efforts and we see a Soviet Union which has built up its counterforce weapons in numbers far greater than our own. If the only reason to develop defensive weapons is to make a disarming first strike possible, then clearly we should be even more concerned that we have been.

We are concerned, and deeply so. But not because you are developing – and unlike us deploying – defensive weaponry. We are concerned over the fact that the Soviet Union for some reason has chosen to deploy a much larger number of weapons suitable for a disarming first strike than has the United States. There may be reasons for this other than actually seeking a first-strike advantage, but we too must look at capabilities rather than intentions. And the fact is that we are certain you have an advantage in this area.

Frankly, you have been misinformed if your specialists say that the missiles on our Trident submarines have a capability to destroy hardened missile silos – a capability your SS-18 definitely has. Current Trident missiles lack the capability for such a role. They could be used only to retaliate. Nor is the Pershing II, which cannot even reach most Soviet strategic weapons, a potential first-strike weapon. Its short flight time is not substantially different from that of the more capable – and much more numerous – Soviet SS 20's aimed at our European allies whom we are pledged to defend and most of whom have no nuclear capability of their own. Our forces currently have a very limited capability to strike Soviet silos, and we are improving this capability only because we cannot accept a situation in which the Soviet Union holds such a clear advantage in counterforce weaponry. Even if we are required to complete all planned deployments in the absences of our accord which limits them, they will not match the number of Soviet weapons with a first-strike capability.

If our defense and military specialists disagree regarding the capability of the weapons on the other side, then by all means let us arrange for them to meet and discuss their concerns. A frank discussion of their respective assessments and the reasons for them could perhaps clear up those misunderstandings which are not based on fact.

In any event, we have both agreed to the principle of a 50% reduction of nuclear arms. Implementing that agreement is surely the first task of our negotiators at Geneva. Let me stress once again that we remain willing to reduce those weapons systems which the Soviet Union finds threatening so long as the Soviet Union will reduce those which pose a special threat to the United States and its allies. Our proposals in November included significant movement on our part in this direction and were a major step to accommodate your concerns. I hope that your negotiators will be empowered to respond to these proposals during the current round and to engage us in identifying which strategic systems are to be included in the 50% reduction.

So far as defensive systems are concerned, I would reiterate what I wrote before: if your concern is that such systems may be used to permit a first-strike strategy, or as a cover for basing weapons of mass destruction in space, then there must be practical ways to prevent such possibilities. Of course I have in mind not general assurances but concrete, verifiable means which both sides can rely on to avoid these contingencies, neither of which is a part of United States strategy or planning. I honestly believe that we can find a solution to this problem if we approach it in a practical fashion rather than debating generalities.

I would like nothing more than to find, by our next meeting, an approach acceptable to both of us to solve this problem. But I believe that will require two things: accelerating negotiations to reach agreement on the way to reduce offensive weapons by 50%, and discussion of concrete ways to insure that any future development of defensive systems cannot be used as a cover for a first-strike strategy or for basing weapons or mass destruction in space. Aside from those broader issues, I believe that your recent proposal brings settlement of the problem of intermediate-range missiles closer and that there are improved measures in several areas.

Regarding regional conflicts, I can see that our respective analysis of the causes are incompatible. There seems little point in continuing to debate those matters on which we are bound to disagree. Instead, I would suggest that we simply look at the current situation in pragmatic terms. Such a look would show two very important facts: that the Soviet Union is engaged in a war in another country and the United States is not. And furthermore, this war is unlikely to bring any benefit to the Soviet Union. So why is it continued?

Certainly not because of the United States. Even if we wished we do not have the power to induce thousands of people to take up arms against a well trained foreign army equipped with the most modern weapons. And neither we nor any country other than the Soviet Union has the power to stop that war. For who can tell the people of another country they should not fight for their motherland, for their independence and their national dignity?

I hope, as you say, that there is an open door to a just political settlement. Of course, we support the U.N. process and hope that it will take a practical and realistic turn. However, 1985 was marked by an intensification of conflict. I can only hope that this is not what the future holds.

As I have said before, if you really want to withdraw from Afghanistan, you will have my cooperation in every reasonable way. We have no desire or intent to exploit a Soviet military withdrawal from Afghanistan to the detriment of Soviet interests. But it is clear that the fighting can be ended only by the withdrawal of Soviet troops, the return of Afghan refugees to their country, and the restoration of a genuinely sovereign, non-aligned state. Such a result would have an immediate positive effect on U.S.-Soviet relations and would help clear the way to progress in many other cases.

The problem of superpower military involvement in local disputes is of course not limited to the tragic conflict in Afghanistan. And I must say candidly that some recent actions by your government are most discouraging. What are we to make of your sharply increased military support of a local dictator who has declared a war of terrorism against much of the rest of the world, and against the United States in particular? How can one take Soviet declarations of opposition to terrorism seriously when confronted with such actions? And more importantly, are we to conclude that the Soviet Union is so reckless in seeking to extend its influence in the world that it will place its prestige (and even the lives of some of its citizens) at the mercy of a mentally unbalanced local despot?

You have made accusations about U.S. policy which I cannot accept. My purpose here, however, is not to debate, but to reach for a way out of the pattern by which one of us becomes militarily involved, directly or indirectly, in local disputes, and thus stimulate the reaction of the other. This transforms what should be of local concern in to a U.S.-Soviet confrontation. As I have said, we believe it is the Soviet Union which has acted without restraint in this respect. You say it is the United States.

But agreement as to who is to blame is not necessary to find a solution. The point I would make is that we must find a way to terminate the military involvement, direct & indirect, of both our countries in these disputes, and avoid spreading such involvement to new areas. This was the goal of the proposal I made last October. Let us encourage the parties to these conflicts to begin negotiations to find political solutions, while our countries support the process by agreeing to terminate the flow of weapons and war material into the area of conflict.

Mr. General Secretary, there remains many points on which we still disagree, and we will probably never reach agreement on some of them. Nevertheless, I am convinced that the critical problems can be solved if we approach them in the proper manner. I have the feeling that we gradually are finding some additional points on which we can agree, and would hope that, by concentrating on practical solutions, we can give greater momentum to this process.

But we do need to speed up the negotiation process if this is going to occur. Therefore, I hope you will instruct your delegations in Geneva, as I have instructed ours, to roll up their sleeves and get seriously to work.

When you announced to the public the ideas contained in your letter of January 14, I made a statement welcoming them. Our study of the message will shortly be completed, and when it is I will be responding specifically to the points you made in it.

Nancy joins me in sending our best regards to you and your wife.

Sincerely,

Ronald Reagan

[Reagan's top-secret response to Gorbachev's January 14 proposal for the complete elimination of nuclear weapons was put on paper in National Security Decision Directive (NSDD) 210, signed February 4, 1986. The top-secret directive explained that the United States agreed in principle to the complete elimination of nuclear weapons, but would no longer negotiate the complete elimination of nuclear weapons because "the total elimination of nuclear weapons requires conditions that include correcting conventional and other force imbalances and problems, full compliance with existing and future treaty obligations, peaceful resolution of regional conflicts in ways that allow free choice without outside interference, and a demonstrated commitment by the Soviet leadership to peaceful competition." Reagan continued in NSDD 210, "The U.S. would also make clear its view that the elimination of nuclear weapons would not obviate the need for defenses against such weapons, particularly to protect against cheating or breakout by any country."

Reagan formally responded to Gorbachev's proposals on February 22. Reagan's counterproposals suggested an overall reduction to 6,000 warheads on strategic delivery vehicles (4,500 on ballistic missiles and 1,500 Air Launched Cruise Missiles (ALCM)); reductions in intermediate range nuclear weapons in Europe while working toward the complete elimination of intermediate range nuclear weapons in Europe; continued research on strategic defense under current ABM Treaty restrictions; Soviet reductions in conventional forces in Europe; initiation of confidence building measures that would make the European "military environment more open, predictable and stable"; and a world-wide ban on the "development, production, possession, and transfer of chemical weapons."

Questions to consider: Was Gorbachev realistic in proposing the complete elimination of nuclear weapons by the year 2000? Should Reagan have agreed? If Reagan had known that the Soviet Union would collapse just a few years later, do you think he would have agreed? Are the arguments presented in NSDD 210 persuasive?

February 22, 1986

Dear Mr. General Secretary,

The elimination of nuclear weapons has been an American goal for decades, from our proposals at the dawn of the nuclear age to my vision of a nuclear-free world made possible through the reliance of our countries on defense rather than on the threat of nuclear retaliation. In a 1983 speech to the Japanese Diet and on many subsequent occasions, I have advocated the abolition of nuclear weapons. I have done so because I believe this is an objective which reflects the deep yearning of people everywhere, and which provides a vision to guide our efforts in the years ahead. It was for similar reasons that I have sought to develop concepts and frameworks to guide the efforts of our governments in other aspects of our relations – whether solving the regional tensions that have damaged our relations over the years, or expanding the people-to-people contacts that can enrich both our societies.

It is in this spirit that I have studied with great care your letter of January 14, your January 15 statement to the Soviet people, and your subsequent statements on the prospects for progress in arms control. I believe they represent a significant and positive step forward.

I am encouraged that you have suggested steps leading toward a world free from nuclear weapons, even though my view regarding the steps necessary differs from yours in certain respects. However, having agreed on the objective and on the need for taking concrete steps to reach that goal, it should be easier to resolve differences in our viewpoints as to what those steps should be. Our initial moves are of course the essential ones to start this process and therefore I believe we should focus our negotiating efforts on them.

Of course, if we are to move toward a world in which the eventual elimination of nuclear weapons will be possible, there must be far greater trust and confidence between our two countries than exists at present. We cannot simply wave away the suspicion and misunderstandings which have developed over the past four decades between our two countries. The process of reducing and eventually eliminating nuclear weapons can by itself nurture greater confidence and trust. But there will be many in my country, and I believe in yours, who will question the wisdom of eliminating nuclear weapons – which both sides see as the ultimate guarantor of their security – if they see the other's conduct as threatening. This leads me to three general observations.

First, it will be vitally necessary as we move down this path to ensure the most stringent verification, with measures far more comprehensive and exacting then in any previous agreement. I welcome your recognition of this in your expressed willingness to make use of on-site inspection and to adopt other measures that may be necessary. For our part, we will be proposing verification procedures tailored to the specific weaponry limits which are contemplated. Our negotiators will, of course, work out the details of the measures, but I believe we both will have to pay close attention to this aspect and see to it that our respective governments develop and implement the necessary arrangements. At the same time, it will be essential to resolve outstanding compliance concerns and ensure that all obligations our governments have undertaken are faithfully observed.

My second point is that any sustained effort to resolve our basic security concerns must go hand-in-hand with concrete steps to move ahead in other areas of our relationship – non-nuclear military issues, regional problems, human rights, and bilateral ties. The buildup of both nuclear and conventional armaments has taken place in recent decades to address perceived threats to security, including conflicts in other regions of the world. Progress on reducing arms should be accompanied by a corresponding effort to deal with these perceptions. The process of eliminating nuclear arms is liable to prove fragile indeed unless we can deal with our competition in a peaceful and responsible way.

I welcome the statement in your January 15 message to the Soviet people, which calls for the settlement of regional conflicts as soon as possible. I would urge you again to consider seriously the proposal I made at the United Nations in October for a comprehensive and flexible framework that would permit our two countries to work together, in conjunction with the peoples involved, to solve regional conflicts that have damaged East-West relations over the years and have brought great suffering to the areas affected. We should make every effort to ensure that in the dialogue on regional issues to which we agreed at Geneva, including discussions by our foreign ministers and the meetings of our senior regional experts, our governments take a fresh look at ways to reduce tensions between us over regional matters. I continue to believe that regional conflicts can and should be resolved peacefully, in ways that allow free choice without outside interference.

Finally, as you know, the United States and its allies must rely today on nuclear weapons to deter conventional as well as nuclear conflict. This is due in large part to the significant imbalance that currently exists between the conventional forces of NATO and the Warsaw Pact. As a result, it would be necessary, as we reduce nuclear weapons toward zero, that we concurrently engage in a process of strengthening the stability of the overall East-West security balance, with particular emphasis on redressing existing conventional imbalances, strengthening confidence-building *measures and accomplishing a verifiable global ban on chemical weapons. In addition, our cooperative efforts to strengthen the nuclear non-proliferation regime would become even more important.*

As for the specifics of your proposal, we certainly agree on the goal of eliminating nuclear weapons as soon as we have achieved the conditions for a world which makes that goal feasible. We also agree on the need to get on with the first steps towards creating those conditions now. The pace of progress towards any target date would have to depend on our ability to arrive at mutually acceptable guarantees to ensure that the security of the United States, the Soviet Union and our respective friends and allies is in no sense diminished along the way.

I also agree that the first steps in moving toward this goal involve deep reductions in the existing arsenals of the United States and the Soviet Union. Also, like you, we can envision subsequent steps which could involve the United Kingdom, France, and the People's Republic of China, so that all can move to zero nuclear weapons in a balanced and stable manner. Finally, I also share the view that our efforts should now focus on the first steps which the U.S. and USSR can take bilaterally to begin the process.

I can also agree with several of your ideas on how this program would proceed. There are other details, however, that would require modification before I could accept them.

For example, as our two nations reduce our nuclear weapons towards zero, it is imperative that we maintain equal limits on those weapons at each stage along the way. To this end, the United States last November proposed a detailed plan for reduction of U.S. and Soviet strategic offensive forces. I am disappointed that the Soviet Union has not yet responded to this proposal, which builds on your ideas presented to me last fall by Foreign Minister Shevardnadze. As we discussed in Geneva, we agree on the principle of deep reductions, but we cannot agree that certain categories of weapons systems on the U.S. side would be included while like weapons on the Soviet side would be excluded.

Similarly, we must insist that limits be based on system capabilities, not expressed intentions. You made this point very eloquently to me in Geneva. In regard to longer-range INF missiles, this means that we cannot exclude systems from limits merely because of their deployment location, since those systems are capable of moving or being transported in a matter of days between different geographic areas.

I have, however, studied closely, your INF proposal of January 15, 1986, and believe that our negotiators at Geneva should be able to arrive at an equitable, verifiable and mutually acceptable INF agreement. In this regard, I have asked our negotiators during this round to propose a concrete plan for the elimination of LRINF missiles, not only in Europe but also in Asia, before the end of 1989.

In the defense and space area, your proposal was ambiguous with regard to strategic defense research. I continue to believe that limits on research could be counterproductive and, in any case, could not be verified; therefore, they must not be included in an agreement. Beyond research, as I suggested in Geneva, if there were no nuclear missiles, then there might also be no need for defenses against them. But I am convinced that some non-nuclear defenses could make a vital contribution to security and stability. In any event, our negotiators in Geneva should thoroughly examine how we could make a transition to a world involving the increasing contribution of such defenses.

With respect to nuclear testing, I believe that, so long as we rely on nuclear weapons as an element of deterrence, we must continue to test in order to ensure their continued safety, security and reliability. However, as I wrote to you in December, I see no reason why we should not consider the matter of nuclear testing as we move forward on other arms control subjects. I suggested we establish a bilateral dialogue aimed at constructive steps in this field. I remain hopeful you will take up this offer.

Finally, although your proposal seems to recognize that the crucial first step is substantial bilateral U.S. and Soviet nuclear reductions, it also attaches certain conditions regarding the forces of the United Kingdom and France. As you know, the United States can make no commitments for other nuclear powers, nor can we agree to bilateral U.S.-Soviet arrangements which would suggest otherwise. The negotiations of limitations on third country nuclear systems is solely the responsibility and prerogative of the governments concerned.

The leaders of Britain, France and China have made known their views on this and on the progress necessary in U.S.-Soviet nuclear reductions and in other arms control areas which would establish the conditions for them to consider how their security interests would be served by participation in future negotiations. Thus, the important task now before us is to make the necessary progress. When we have done so – as I noted earlier – I can envision a process involving the other nuclear powers, so that we all can move to zero nuclear weapons in a balanced and stable manner.

With these considerations in mind, and building upon your proposal, I propose that we agree upon the elements which we hold in common, as outlined above, and that we accelerate work on the first bilateral steps. Implementing details must be worked out by our negotiators in Geneva, Vienna, and Stockholm, but our guiding objective should be to reach meaningful, verifiable and balanced arms control measures, each of which can stand on its merits at every stage of the larger process.

In summary, I would propose that the process toward our agreed goal of eliminating nuclear weapons include the following elements:

Initial Steps. I believe that these steps should involve reduction in and limits on nuclear, conventional, and chemical weapons as follows:

1. *The U.S. and USSR would reduce the number of warheads on their strategic ballistic missiles to 4500 and the number of ALCMs on their heavy bombers to 1500 resulting in no more than a total number of 6000 such warheads on strategic nuclear delivery vehicles. These reductions would be carried out in such a way as to enhance stability.*

2. *In the INF area, by 1987 both the United States and the Soviet Union would limit their LRINF missile deployments in Europe to no more than 140 launchers each, with the Soviet Union making concurrent, proportionate reductions in Asia. Within the following year, both sides would further reduce the numbers of LRINF launchers remaining in Europe and Asia by an additional 50%. Finally, both sides would move to the total elimination of this category of weapons by the end of 1989.*

3. *Research programs on strategic defenses would be conducted in accordance with treaty obligations.*

4. *The U.S. and the USSR would establish an effective MBFR verification regime and carry out initial reductions in manpower levels along the lines of the recent Western proposal at the MBFR negotiations; they would then begin a process of moving on to a balance of non-nuclear capabilities in Europe.*

5. *Concrete and meaningful confidence-building measures designed to make the European military environment more open, predictable, and stable would be initiated.*

6. *An effective, comprehensive worldwide ban on the development, production, possession, and transfer of chemical weapons would be instituted, with strict verification measures including international on-site inspection.*

Subsequent Steps. Subsequent steps could involve other nuclear powers and would aim at further reductions and increasingly strict limits, ultimately leading to the elimination of all nuclear weapons. We would embark on this process as soon as the steps encompassed in the first stage are completed. The goal would be to complete the process as soon as the conditions for a non-nuclear world had been achieved.

Obligations assumed in all steps and areas would be verified by national technical means, by on-site inspection as needed, and by such additional measures as might prove necessary.

I hope that this concept provides a mutually acceptable route to a goal that all the world shares. I look forward to your response and to working with you in the coming months in advancing this most important effort.

Let me conclude by agreeing with you that we should work constructively before your visit to the United States to prepare concrete agreements on the full range of issues we discussed at Geneva. Neither of us has illusions about the major problems, which remain between our two countries, but I wish to assure you that I am determined to work with you energetically in finding practical solutions to those problems. I agree with you that we should use our correspondence as a most important channel of communication in preparing for your visit.

Nancy and I would like to extend to you, Mrs. Gorbacheva and your family our best wishes. It is our hope that this year will bring significant progress toward our mutual goal of building a better relationship between our two countries, and a safer world.

Sincerely,

Ronald Reagan

[Reagan's public calls for the elimination of nuclear weapons proved Prime Minister Thatcher correct. Two-years earlier she privately conveyed to him her worry that his calls for the elimination of nuclear weapons would significantly hurt hers and his chances when it came time for them to ask their governments to continue to support their outlandish defense budget requests. Reagan, as Thatcher predicted, was now faced with a congress about to reject his defense budget request. The president responded by taking to his favorite medium, the television, to plead his case directly to the American people. "I will never ask for what isn't needed," Reagan told Americans in a nationally televised prime-time address. "I will never fight for what isn't necessary. But I need your help. We've come so far together these last five years; let's not falter now. Let's maintain that crucial level of national strength, unity, and purpose that has brought the Soviet Union to the negotiating table and has given us this historic opportunity to achieve real reductions in nuclear weapons and a real chance at lasting peace."]

April 2, 1986

Dear Mr. President,

I have requested A.F. Dobrynin to transmit this letter to you personally as a follow-up to our exchange of views.

I would like to say that we value A.F. Dobrynin's long years of activity as Soviet ambassador to Washington and his vigorous efforts to develop mutual understanding between our two nations. This, of course, has been greatly facilitated by the contacts he maintained with the American leadership, including under your Administration. We hope that similar opportunities will be available to his successor who we are currently selecting and who will be named shortly.

I intend to send you a more detailed letter on a number of specific issues in our relations and also amplifying on those ideas that I have set forth below. Now, I would like to share with you some of my general observations that I have, and, surely, you must have your own, regarding the state and prospects of the relationship between our two countries. I believe, in doing so, one has to use as a point of departure our meeting in Geneva where we both assumed certain obligations.

I think our assessments of that meeting coincide: it was necessary and useful, it introduced a certain stabilizing element to the relations between the USSR and the USA and to the world situation in general. It was only natural that it also generated no small hopes for the future.

More than four months have passed since the Geneva meeting. We ask ourselves: what is the reason for things not going the way they, it would seem, should have gone? Where is the real turn for the better? We, within the Soviet leadership, regarded the Geneva meeting as a call for translating understandings of principle reached there into specific actions with a view to giving an impetus to our relations and to building up their positive dynamics. And we have been doing just that after Geneva.

With this in mind, we have put forward a wide-ranging and concrete program of measures concerning the limitation and reduction of arms and disarmament. It is from the standpoint of new approaches to seeking mutually acceptable solutions that the Soviet delegations have acted in Geneva, Vienna and Stockholm.

What were the actions of the USA? One has to state, unfortunately, that so far the positions have not been brought closer together so that it would open up a real prospect for reaching agreements. I will not go into details or make judgments of the US positions here. But there is one point I would like to make. One gathers the impression that all too frequently attempts are being made to portray our initiatives as propaganda, as a desire to score high points in public opinion or as a wish to put the other side into an awkward position. We did not and do not harbor such designs. After all, our initiatives can be easily tested for their practicality. Our goal is to reach agreement, to find solutions to problems which concern the USSR, the USA and actually all other countries.

I have specifically focused on this matter so as to ensure a correct, unbiased and business-like treatment of our proposals. I am sure that it will make it easier to reach agreement.

Now what has been taking place in the meantime outside the negotiations? Of course, each of us has his own view of the policy of the other side. But here again, has the Soviet Union done anything in foreign affairs or bilateral relations that would contribute to mounting tensions or be detrimental to the legitimate interests of the USA? I can say clearly: no, there has been nothing of that sort.

On the other hand, we hear increasingly vehement philippics addressed to the USSR and are also witnessing quite a few actions directly aimed against our interests and, to put it frankly, against our relations becoming more stable and constructive. All this builds suspicion with regard to the US policy, and, surely, creates no favorable backdrop for the summit meeting. I am saying it with no ambiguity in order to avoid in this regard any uncertainties or misunderstanding that only one side should exercise restraint and display a positive attitude. Our relations take shape not in a vacuum, their general atmosphere is a wholly material concept. The calmer the atmosphere, the easier it is to solve issues which are of equal concern to both sides.

The issues have to be solved – there is no doubt about it. And above all this bears on the area of security. You are familiar with our proposals, they cover all the most important aspects. At the same time I would like specifically to draw your attention to the fact that we do not say: all or nothing. We are in favor of moving forward step by step and we outlined certain possibilities in this regard, particularly, at the negotiations on nuclear and space arms.

We maintained a serious and balanced approach to the problem of ending nuclear tests. One would not want to lose hope that we shall succeed in finding a practical solution to this issue in the way that the world expects us to do. It is hardly necessary to point out the importance of this matter as it is. The solution thereof carries with it also a great positive political potential. It is precisely one of the central thoughts contained in the message of the Delhi Six – countries which called for building a favorable atmosphere in the relations between the USSR and the USA and in the international situation as a whole. We took that also into account, having reacted positively to their appeal to our countries not to conduct nuclear tests pending the next Soviet-American summit meeting.

It was the desire that we work together in the cessation of nuclear tests and set a good example to all nuclear powers that motivated my recent proposal for both of us to meet specifically on this issue at one of the European capitals. Have another look at this proposal, Mr. President, in a broad political context. I repeat, what is meant here is a specific, single-purpose meeting. Such a meeting, of course, would not be a substitute for the new major meeting that we agreed upon in Geneva.

I do very serious thinking with regard to the latter, first of all with a view to making that meeting truly meaningful and substantial, so that it should enable us to move closer to putting into practice the fundamental understandings reached in Geneva. As you know, I have mentioned one of the questions pertaining to the area of security which are worthwhile working on in preparing for our meeting. I reaffirm that we are ready to seek here solutions in a most serious way, which would be mutually acceptable and not detrimental to the security of either side. Given the mutual will it would be also possible to ascertain other possibilities for agreement in the context of the forthcoming meeting both in the area of space and nuclear arms and on the issues discussed in other fora. To be sure, we also have things to discuss as far as regional matters are concerned.

I assume that you are also working on all these questions and in the subsequent correspondence we will be able in a more specific and substantive way to compare our mutual preliminary ideas for the purpose of bringing the positions closer together. Obviously, this joint work, including the preparations for our meeting, will benefit from the exchanges of views at other levels and particularly from the forthcoming contacts between our Foreign Minister and your Secretary of State.

I will be looking forward with interest to hearing from you.

Sincerely,

M. GORBACHEV

["We must talk about a reply to this," Reagan noted after reading the letter. The president's reply came the following week.]

April 11, 1986

Dear Mr. General Secretary:

Thank you for your letter of April 2, which Ambassador Dobrynin delivered. As Ambassador Dobrynin will report to you, your letter served as the point of departure for a very useful meeting we held in my office, and for additional meetings between him and Secretary Shultz. It is clear that both of us are concerned about the relative lack of progress since our meeting in Geneva in moving overall relations in a positive direction. While each of us would cite quite different reasons to explain this situation, I agree with your thought that the important thing now is to focus attention on how we can solve the concrete problems facing us.

I described to Ambassador Dobrynin a number of goals which I believe we could set for our meeting. This was of course an optimum list. I recognize that achieving these goals will be a complex and difficult process and that we may not be able to achieve them all in the immediate future. I am confident, however, that all can be achieved if we have the will to get to work on them promptly. Furthermore, they are sufficiently important that progress on even a few of them would be a worthwhile achievement.

Although I believe we should not relent in our search for ways to bridge critical differences between our countries, I agree with your observation on the desirability of moving step by step when an overall solution to a problem eludes us. I want to assure you that our proposals, like yours, are not "all or nothing at all." We wish to negotiate, to find compromises that serve the interests of each of us, and to achieve as much progress as possible. If we can make a critical breakthrough, that of course would be best. But as we attempt to deal with the key issues, we should simultaneously try to solve as many of the smaller ones as we can in order to develop momentum for dealing successfully with the larger issues.

This applies particularly to the nuclear testing issue, which you mentioned in your letter. Since nuclear testing occurs because we both depend on nuclear weapons for our security, our ability eventually to eliminate testing is intimately connected with our ability to agree on ways to reduce and eventually eliminate nuclear weapons themselves. This is why we simply cannot enter into the moratorium you have proposed.

However, there must be practical means by which we can begin resolving our differences on this issue. Congressmen Fascell and Broomfield have reported to me your suggestion that we open a dialogue to discuss both your ideas and ours on this subject. I am prepared to agree to this idea, to have our representatives meet to discuss the principal concerns on both sides without preconditions. If we could agree on concrete verification improvements for the Threshold Test Ban Treaty and Treaty on Peaceful Nuclear Explosions, we would be prepared to support ratification of those treaties and create conditions which would let us move toward our ultimate goal of banning all tests.

I have taken careful note of your suggestion that we meet in Europe to deal with this issue. While I agree that it is very important, it is hard for me to understand the basis for a meeting on our level, devoted solely to this issue, when it has been impossible to arrange for our representatives to discuss it. In any event, our calendars are such that we would be able to arrange the meeting we agreed on in Geneva as soon and as easily as we could arrange a one-purpose meeting in Europe. Wouldn't it be better to treat this issue first at a lower level, in the hope that a way could be found to produce some concrete result when we meet in the United States?

In addition to the substantive suggestions I made to Ambassador Dobrynin, I asked him to convey to you some ideas for procedures we *might follow to speed up resolution of the issues we face. I hope you will give them serious consideration.*

I am pleased that Secretary Shultz and Foreign Minister Shevardnadze will be meeting in May to discuss how we can accelerate the preparations for your visit to the U.S. I would hope, however, that we can begin immediately to exchange ideas regarding practical goals we can set, and therefore look forward to receiving your more detailed letter and your reaction to the ideas I presented to Ambassador Dobrynin. I would also like to suggest that you look again at our most recent arms control proposals – the comprehensive proposal of November 1 and the INF proposal of February 24. I believe there are positive elements in them on which we can build. Both of these proposals were designed to pick up on positive aspects of your proposals and bridge the previous positions of our two sides. They also would provide key elements in implementing the first phase of your proposal of January 15.

In conclusion, I want to convey to you the high regard in which Ambassador Dobrynin is held in our country. He has played a truly distinguished, historic role in relations between our two countries for over two decades, and we view his departure from Washington with regret. I understand, however, that his future duties will involve relations between our countries, so that we look forward to working with him in the future as well.

I am certain that Ambassador Dobrynin's successor will be received by American officials and our public with the respect due the representative of a great nation. I agree with you that the widest possible contacts by our Ambassador both in Washington and Moscow are important if we are to achieve a greater measure of mutual understanding.

Nancy joins me in sending our warn personal regards to you and Mrs. Gorbacheva.

Sincerely,
Ronald Reagan

May 23, 1986

Dear Mr. General Secretary,

Since my last letter, a number of events have occurred which neither of us could have predicted. Therefore, it may be useful for you to have my personal thoughts on how we might set relations between our countries in a more positive direction.

Let me begin by expressing my admiration for the courage with which the Soviet people have responded to the recent tragedy at Chernobyl. Dr. Gale has described to us in stirring detail the sacrifices and skill with which your experts are dealing with the human and physical consequences of the disaster. We wish you success in your efforts. Our hearts go out to those Soviet citizens who have been affected by this tragedy. We offer our condolences to the families of those who perished and our good wished for the recovery and well-being of others affected. We remain ready to help in dealing with the consequences of the tragedy if this is desired.

In your address on May 14, 1986, you made some constructive suggestions for international cooperation in dealing with the safety of nuclear power plants. I agree with you that such action is highly desirable. You will have the full cooperation of the United States in working for effective international arrangements in this area. I would propose that Ambassador Kenney and Chairman Petrosyants be prepared to discuss in detail what form such cooperation might take when they next meet.

Mr. General Secretary, it is time to put behind us any misunderstandings arising out of the accident at Chernobyl. I regret that you misinterpreted the motives behind our offers of assistance. Unfortunately, this misunderstanding is all too characteristic of the recent dynamics of our relationship. Following our meeting last fall, I wanted to build on the momentum I felt we had established. I thought we had agreed to accelerate progress in achieving the very specific goals we had set for ourselves. That was why I instructed Secretary Shultz to propose early dates for our next meeting.

In the absence of a response to our proposal, I have sought to communicate to you in our private correspondence, during Secretary Dobrynin's recent visit, and through diplomatic channels specific ideas on what the outcome of a 1986 meeting might be I described to Secretary Dobrynin, for example, our readiness to reach agreement by the next summit on the key elements of treaties to reduce strategic nuclear forces and eliminate intermediate range nuclear missiles, as well as on methods to remove both the threat of an effective first strike from either side and the use of space for basing weapons of mass destruction. I also indicated that I was prepared for our experts to meet to discuss the important issue of nuclear testing. As you know, we feel that effective verification is the key to further progress in this area, but we are prepared, of course, to give careful consideration to any proposals you wish to advance.

We have, in short, made a good faith effort to set in motion the serious, high-level discussions necessary to prepare for a meeting between us. I regret that it has not been possible to begin them. While there have been positive steps in some areas, we have lost a full six months in dealing with *the issues which most merit our personal attention. I hope you will agree that it is time to concentrate on the agenda we set forth in Geneva last November.*

I am prepared to do my part. As I have said, I am eager to achieve tangible practical results at our next meeting. I agree with you that an atmosphere conducive to progress is important. The suggestions I have made, which took careful account of your comments to me on the issues, sought to find a mutually acceptable approach to some of the key issues.

The atmosphere of our relationship is also affected, of course, by what the two of us say publicly. The approach I intend to take in my public statements is to reaffirm my strong personal commitment to achieve concrete progress in all the areas of our relationship during the remaining years of my administration. I hope that in our correspondence we can begin to make such progress.

I would also propose that we arrange for our Foreign Ministers to meet to review these critical matters as soon as possible. If it is more convenient for Minister Shevardnadze to have the meeting in Europe than in Washington, that would be acceptable to us.

Mr. General Secretary, our recent history provides ample evidence that, if we wait for an ideal moment to try to resolve our differences, we are unlikely to resolve anything. This is the moment which has been given to us. We should take advantage of it since it is a time of historic and possibly unique potential. Let us not lose it for lack of effort.

Sincerely yours,
Ronald Reagan

June 1, 1986
Text of General Secretary's address to the CPSU Central Committee

In my television address of May 14, I touched upon the main conclusions that we believe can be drawn from the accident at Chernobyl. Today I wish to share with you some additional thoughts on this matter.

It is quite obvious that there is a practical need to begin establishing without delay an international system for the safe development of nuclear energy. Such a system would be directed toward reducing to an absolute minimum the possibility of the peaceful atom causing harm to people. Guaranteeing the reliable, safe development of nuclear energy should become the universal, international obligation of each and every state.

Preliminary steps in this direction are already being taken, including those by the IAEA. Individual states are setting forth various ideas and proposals. We are giving them careful consideration.

I should like to say at the outset that we do not claim to possess ready-made solutions. A total of 152 accidents at atomic power stations involving the release of radioactivity have been recorded throughout the world; thus, a number of states have experience in this area, and an international system for nuclear safety should be worked out on the basis of this experience.

Of course, the first thing we need is a system of prompt notification in the event of accidents and malfunctions at nuclear power plants when such occurrences are accompanied by the release of radiation. The notification is also connected with the problem of obtaining data when there are possible deviations in levels of natural background radioactivity.

Many states are unable to cope with a nuclear accident with their own resources. Therefore, we believe that it is vital that an international system for safe developments of nuclear energy include an efficient mechanism for providing mutual assistance as quickly as possible when dangerous situations arise. Both the IAEA and the World Health Organization could contribute to such a mechanism. Any efforts to eliminate the consequences of a nuclear accident should involve not only the state in whose territory it occurred but also other states, if their assistance is requested.

There is also the question of the legal form of agreements concerning the system of notification and the mechanism for providing assistance. It seems to us that the relevant obligations of states could be set forth and stipulated in a special international convention or conventions. The Soviet side is presently considering all these questions and, taking into account the proposals of other states, will submit its ideas on this subject.

Some states, while agreeing to this solution of the problem, have asked that pending a convention, a decision be reached as early as June regarding the establishment in the IAEA of a system of notification in the event of a nuclear accident. Well, the sooner we can take appropriate measures – even if they are of a preliminary, temporary nature – the better.

At the same time, we think our main task is to take measures which would guarantee the prevention of accidents. This can be done by submitting information to the IAEA on the causes of accidents as expeditiously as is practically feasible. Such information would be studied by appropriate specialists to help the IAEA member countries take into account the given experience for the purpose of further increasing the safety of nuclear energy.

Further steps ought to be taken as well, such as formulating recommendations in the IAEA on the safety of nuclear power plants, and strengthening national and, where necessary, international controls to enforce them in all states. The leading nuclear countries could also be made to cooperate, under IAEA auspices, in creating a new generation of economical and reliable reactors that will be safer to operate than the existing reactors.

We must also take into account the fact that the financial and psychological damage resulting from accidents at nuclear power plants and installations have not been studied adequately on an international scale. We believe that these matters must be properly regulated to prevent and eliminate attempts to use nuclear accidents to exacerbate tensions and foment distrust in relations between states.

I think the problem of standardizing the permissible levels of radiation adopted by various countries deserve further study.

Now should we overlook another aspect of nuclear safety – prevention of nuclear terrorism. One cannot help but be concerned about the acts of sabotage committed against nuclear power facilities in the West. There were thirty-two incidents of sabotage in the United States between 1974 and 1984, and then such incidents in Europe between 1966 and 1977. The inadequacy of measures to prevent the theft of highly enriched fissionable material is also a cause for concern. This however, is far from an exhaustive list of the possibilities that terrorists have. In light of these facts, we think the time has come to work out a reliable system of measures to prevent nuclear terrorism in all its manifestations.

In establishing an international system for the safe development of nuclear energy we can use the available resources of various international agencies – the IAEA, the World Health Organization, UNEP, the World Meteorological Organization, and the United Nations. All this must be placed on a permanent basis of broad international cooperation.

The IAEA should of course be the main link in this system. Therefore it would be advisable to enlarge the role and responsibilities of this agency. Obviously it will be necessary to increase its financial and material capabilities for this purpose. This problem could be resolved, for example, by allocating special mandatory contributions from the interested member states of the agency. Some thought might also be given to creating a special fund in the IAEA for providing emergency assistance in the event of a nuclear accident for those countries which may require it.

On May 14 I suggested already that a high-level international conference be convened in Vienna, under the auspices of the IAEA, to discuss all these issues.

I should like to tell you that we are taking concrete steps to improve the work of the USSR State Committee for safety in the Atomic Power Industry, which was established several years ago. We intend to expand its ties with the corresponding international organizations as well as with similar national agencies in order to exchange experiences in regulating the safe development of nuclear energy.

Let me also add that we are making a thorough analysis of our nuclear energy program, and are working on and shall implement measures to increase the operational safety of nuclear power plants, on the basis of the conclusions we have drawn from the Chernobyl accident.

I should like to emphasize once more that the lessons learned from this accident should benefit all mankind. What occurred at Chernobyl serves as a serious reminder of the terrible forces contained in the energy of the atom. If an accident at a peaceful nuclear power plant turned into a disaster, one can imagine the tragic consequences for all mankind that would results from the use of nuclear weapons, which exist precisely for the purpose of destruction and annihilation.

The nuclear-space age requires new political thinking and new policies from the leaders of all countries. These inexorably severe demands are met by the program proposed by us for the complete elimination of nuclear weapons and the creation of a comprehensive system of international security.

Ever since the appearance of nuclear weapons, the best minds have pondered how to recork the nuclear jinni. But in the meantime the nuclear arms race has intensified. Where is the key, the decisive link with which the nuclear problem can be resolved? The cessation of nuclear testing could become the first practical step toward nuclear disarmament. We attach great importance to this measure, for it is quite effective and easy to implement. Simply stop nuclear testing – under strict controls, of course. This measure should finally become a reality of international life.

By extending its unilateral ban on nuclear explosions, the Soviet Union has agreed not to carry them out in essence for an entire year. We believe that such a protracted period of time should prove more than enough for the American side to thoroughly weigh the situation and take equivalent measures that will make it possible to end nuclear testing on a bilateral basis.

In view of the extraordinary aspect of the problem of stopping nuclear testing, I have repeated my offer to President Reagan to hold a meeting without delay and come to an agreement on a nuclear test ban.

Both these tasks – the safeguarding of the peaceful use of nuclear energy, and feeing our planet from nuclear weapons – require broad international interaction and the joint efforts of all states and particularly of international nuclear agencies and public entities interested in creating a comprehensive and reliable system of international security. This is the concern of all states, severally and jointly. We call upon you to contribute to this important cause, on which depends the preservation of human civilization.

July 25, 1986

Dear Mr. General Secretary,

I have taken careful note of the proposals your negotiators made during the recent round in Geneva. I have also continued to ponder our discussion in Geneva last November and our subsequent correspondence, including your June 19th *letter. As you may have guessed from our earlier exchanges, I heartily agree with the statement you made in your address to the last plenary session of the CPSU Central Committee about the need to "search for new approaches to make it possible to clear the road to a reduction of nuclear arms." That is certainly the most urgent task before us.*

In Geneva, you expressed to me your concern that one side might acquire the capability to deliver a disarming first strike against the other by adding advanced strategic defenses to a larger arsenal of offensive nuclear weapons. The United States does not possess the numbers of weapons needed to carry out an effective first strike; nor do we have any intention of acquiring such a capability. Quite the contrary, you well know my strong view that we both should immediately and significantly reduce the size of our nuclear arsenals. Nevertheless, since this remains a particular concern from your point of view, I agree that the "new approach" you have called for should address this concern directly. Neither side should have a first strike capability.

We have both focused on the issue of advanced systems of strategic defense in connection with a "new approach." Research and exploration on the feasibility of such advanced strategic defenses is a subject we have discussed together. I want to address it now, at the very outset of this letter, because I am aware that this is a matter of great concern to both of us. We both agree that neither side should deploy systems of strategic defense simply to augment and enhance its offensive capability. I have assured you that the United States has no interest in seeking unilateral advantage in this area. To ensure that neither of us is in a position to do so, we would be prepared immediately to conclude an agreement incorporating the following limits:

(a) While it may take longer to complete such research, both sides would confine themselves for five years, through 1991, to a program of research, development and testing, which is permitted by the ABM Treaty, to determine whether, in principle, advanced reliable systems of strategic defense are technically feasible. Such research and development could include testing necessary to establish feasibility. In the event either side wishes to conduct such testing, the other side shall have the right to observe the tests, in accord with mutually agreed procedures.

(b) Following this five year period, or at some later future time, either the United States or the Soviet Union may determine that advanced systems of strategic defense are technically feasible. Either party may then desire to proceed beyond research, development, and testing to deployment of an advanced strategic defense system. In anticipation that this may occur, we would be prepared to sign a treaty now which would require the party that decides to proceed to deploy an advanced strategic defense system to share the benefits of such a systems with the other providing there is mutual agreement to eliminate the offensive ballistic missiles of both sides. Once a plan is offered to this end, the details of the sharing arrangement and the elimination of offensive ballistic missiles would be the subject of negotiations for a period of no more than two years.

(c) If, following the initial five year period and subsequent to two years after either side has offered a plan for such sharing and the associated mutual elimination of ballistic missiles, the United States and Soviet Union have not agreed on such a plan, either side will be free to deploy unilaterally after six months notice of such intentions is given to the other side.

You also continue to express concern that research on advanced defensive systems could lead to the deployment of spaceborne systems designed to inflict mass destruction on earth. This is certainly not our intention, and I do not agree that such an outcome is a necessary result of such reason. We already are both party to agreements in force that address this subject. And, quite the contrary to your concern, U.S. research into advanced defenses is focused on finding ways to defend directly against offensive ballistic missiles that transit through space and are specifically designed to produce such mass destruction. However, in the context of the approach outlined above, I would also be prepared to have our representatives discuss additional assurances that would further ban deployment in space of advanced weapons capable of inflicting mass destruction on the surface of the earth.

I believe you would agree that significant commitments of this type with respect to strategic defenses would make sense only if made in conjunction with the implementation of immediate actions on both sides to begin moving toward our common goal of the total elimination of nuclear weapons. Toward this goal, I believe we also share the view that the process must begin with radical and stabilizing reductions in the offensive nuclear arsenals of both the United States and the Soviet Union.

In the area of strategic offensive nuclear forces, we remain concerned about what we perceive as a first-strike capability against at least a portion of our retaliatory forces. This is a condition that I cannot ignore. I continue to hope that our efforts in pursuit of significant reductions in existing nuclear arsenals will help resolve this problem. I remain firmly committed to our agreement to seek the immediate implementation of the principle of a fifty percent reduction, on an equitable and verifiable basis, of existing strategic arsenals of the United States and the Soviet Union. The central provision should be reduction of strategic ballistic missile warheads. However, if necessary, I am prepared to consider initial reductions of a less sweeping nature as an interim measure. In this context, along with specific limits on ballistic missile warheads, we are prepared to limit long-range air-launched cruise missiles to below our current plan, and to limit the total number of ICBMs, SLBMs and heavy bombers to a level in the range suggested by the Soviet side. Such reductions should take into account differences among systems in a manner which enhances stability. These reductions should begin as soon as possible and be completed within in agreed period of time.

At the same time, we could deal with the question of intermediate-range nuclear missiles by agreeing on the goal of eliminating this entire class of land-based, LRINF missiles world-wide, which is consistent with the total elimination of all nuclear weapons, and by agreeing on immediate steps that would lead toward this goal in either one step, or, if you prefer, in a series of steps. Your comments regarding intermediate range nuclear missile systems suggest to me that we were heading in the right direction last November when we endorsed the idea of an interim INF agreement. While an immediate agreement leading to the elimination of long range INF missiles systems throughout the world would be the best outcome, an interim approach, on a global basis, may prove the most promising way to achieve early reductions.

Both sides have now put forward proposals whose ultimate result would be equality at zero for our two countries in long range INF missile warheads. If we can also agree that such equality is possible at a level above zero, we would take a major step towards the achievement of an INF agreement.

We should seek such an interim agreement without delay. I would be interested in any specific suggestions that you may wish to offer towards this end. It is important that reductions begin immediately and that significant progress can be achieved within an agreed period of time.

Of course, I hope that we can also agree now that once we have achieved a fifty percent reduction in the U.S. and Soviet strategic arsenals and make progress in eliminating long-range INF missiles, we would continue to pursue negotiations for further stabilizing reductions. The overall aim should be the elimination of all nuclear weapons.

I will be instructing our negotiators to present these proposals, along with appropriate implementing details, when the next round of negotiations begin in Geneva in September. I hope that your negotiators will be prepared to respond in a positive and constructive fashion so that we can proceed promptly to agreement.

Mr. General Secretary, I hope that you will notice that I have tried explicitly to take into account the concerns you expressed to me in Geneva and in our correspondence, as well as key elements of your recent proposals. I believe you will see that this approach provides assurance that neither country would be able to exploit research on strategic defense to acquire a disarming first-strike capability, or to deploy weapons of mass destruction in space. The framework I propose should permit us to proceed immediately to reduce existing nuclear arsenals as we have agreed is desirable, and to establish the conditions for proceeding to further reductions toward the goal of total elimination.

With respect to nuclear testing, as you know, we believe a safe, reliable and effective nuclear deterrent requires testing. Thus, while a ban on such testing remains a long-term U.S. objective, I cannot see how we could move immediately to a complete ban on such testing under present circumstances. We are, however, hopeful that with the initiation of discussions between our respective experts, we can make progress toward eliminating the verification uncertainties which currently preclude ratification of the treaties signed in 1974 and 1976.

Upon ratification of these treaties, and in association with a program to reduce and eliminate nuclear weapons, we would be prepared to discuss ways to implement a parallel program to achieve progress in effectively limiting and ultimately eliminating nuclear testing in a step-by-step fashion. The immediate next step is our agreement on verification procedures which would permit ratification of the 1974 and 1976 treaties. I would hope that the exchanges between our experts will permit us to take this step promptly.

With regard to conventional and chemical forces, I fully agree that the existing fora and channels should be used more actively. As you know, it is our view that the correction of conventional and other force imbalances is one of the vital requirements for achieving the complete elimination of nuclear weapons. Confidential exchanges between our negotiators and experts, away from the glare of publicity, might be useful. I would suggest that such discussions could first profit by preliminary exchanges to clarify and focus the agenda of such meetings. When we have been able to make some preliminary progress on this point, we may wish to consider having our respective ambassadors to the negotiations in Vienna and Stockholm, and at the Committee on Disarmament in Geneva, get together in capitals for bilateral exchanges.

It will be particularly important to ensure a successful conclusion of the Conference on Disarmament in Europe before the CSCE review conference convenes in Vienna. We are seriously considering your recent proposals for limiting conventional weapons in Europe. A more forthcoming response by the Warsaw Pact to the NATO proposal of last December in the MBFR negotiations in Vienna would be helpful.

Regarding other issues, I agree with you that a number of possibilities exist for joint action. You have my earlier message regarding nuclear power plant safety, and I am pleased that our representatives are working actively in the International Atomic Energy Agency to develop more effective means of international cooperation. The exploration of space is also a potentially fruitful area for U.S.-Soviet cooperation, and I would propose that our specialists meet soon to discuss the possibilities of an agreement in this area.

Your proposal for organizing our work in the coming weeks seems sound to me. We have already agreed on several meetings by specialists, and we look forward to consultations with one of your Deputy Foreign Ministers shortly. Should either of us consider other meetings by specialists desirable, we should be able to arrange these, as needed, through normal diplomatic channels. Thus, it would appear that Secretary Shultz and Foreign Minister Shevardnadze will have a well prepared agenda when they meet in September.

There are, of course, a number of important questions in addition to those I have mentioned in this letter which we must continue to address if we are to create the most propitious conditions for your visit to the United States. I believe we have now established a framework to deal with them, and I hope that we can move rapidly toward that "decisive turn" in relations between our countries which we both agree is overdue.

Sincerely,

Ronald Reagan

September 4, 1986

Dear Mr. General Secretary,

I am sure that you have been monitoring, as I have, developments relating to the detention by Soviet authorities of the U.S. News and World Report Moscow correspondent, Nicholas Daniloff. I would like you to have in mind two points as you consider how to handle this case.

First, I can give you my personal assurance that Mr. Daniloff has no connection whatever with the U.S. Government. If you have been informed otherwise, you have been misinformed.

Second, there are no grounds for Mr. Daniloff's detention, nor for any attempt to link him to any other case. If he is not freed promptly, it can only have the most serious and far-reaching consequences for the relationship between our two countries. That would be an extremely unfortunate outcome, and I therefore thought it important to emphasize personally the gravity with which this situation is viewed by the United States.

Therefore, I hope sincerely you will take the necessary actions to allow us to put this matter behind us in the nearest future.

Sincerely,

Ronald Reagan

September 6, 1986

Dear Mr. President,

Your letter of September 5 prompted me to ask for information regarding the questions you raised. As was reported to me by the competent authorities, Daniloff, the Moscow correspondent of the U.S. New and World Report magazine had for a long time been engaged in impermissible activities damaging to the state interests of the USSR. Now an investigation is being conducted by the results of which we shall be able to make a conclusive judgment about this entire case.

I think that we both should not permit the use of questions of such kind to the detriment of the Soviet-American relations whose improvement and development are extremely important.

Sincerely,

M. GORBACHEV

September 15, 1986

Dear Mr. President,

I chose to send this letter with E.A. Shevardnadze, who is leaving for the United States to attend the session of the United Nations General Assembly. He is also planning, as has been agreed, to visit Washington and to discuss thoroughly the questions of interest to both sides.

After we received your letter of July 25, 1986, which has been given careful consideration, certain developments and incidents of a negative nature have taken place. This is yet another indication of how sensitive relations between the USSR and the United States are and how important it is for the top leaders of the two countries to keep them constantly within view and exert a stabilizing influence whenever the amplitude of their fluctuations becomes threatening.

Among such incidents – of the kind that have happened before and that, presumably, no one can be guaranteed against in the future – is the case of Zakharov and Daniloff. It requires a calm examination, investigation, and a search for mutually acceptable solutions. However, the US side has unduly dramatized that incident. A massive hostile campaign has been launched against our country, which has been taken up at the higher levels of the United States administration and Congress. It is as if a pretext was deliberately sought to aggravate Soviet-American relations and to increase tension.

A question then arises: what about the atmosphere so needed for the normal course of negotiations and certainly for preparing and holding the summit meeting?

Since the Geneva meeting, the Soviet Union has been doing a great deal to ensure that the atmosphere is favorable and that negotiations make possible practical preparations for our meeting.

On the major issues of limiting and reducing arms – nuclear, chemical and conventional – we have undertaken intensive efforts in a search for concrete solutions aimed at radically reducing the level of military confrontation in a context of equivalent security.

However, Mr. President, in the spirit of candidness which is coming to characterize our dialogue, I have to tell you that the overall character of US actions in international affairs, the positions on which its representatives insist at negotiations and consultations, and the content of your letter, all give rise to grave and disturbing thoughts. One has to conclude that in effect no start has been made in implementing the agreements we reached in Geneva on improving Soviet-American relations, accelerating the negotiations on nuclear and space arms, and renouncing attempts to secure military superiority. Both in letters and publicly we have made known our views as to the causes of such development, and for my part I do not want to repeat here our assessment of the situation.

First of all, a conclusion comes to mind: is the U.S. leadership at all prepared and really willing to seek agreements which would lead to the termination of the arms race and to genuine disarmament? It is a fact, after all, that despite vigorous efforts by the Soviet side we will have still not moved an inch closer to an agreement on arms reduction.

Having studied your letter and the proposals contained therein, I began to think where they would lead in terms of seeking solutions.

First. You are proposing that we should agree that the ABM Treaty continue to exist for another five-to-seven years, while activities to destroy it would go ahead. Thus, instead of making headway, there would be some thing that complicates even what has been achieved.

We have proposed that any work on anti-missile systems be confined to laboratories. In response, we witness attempts to justify the development of space weapons and their testing at test sites, and declarations, made in advance, of the intention to start in five-to-seven years deploying large-scale ABM systems and thus to nullify the Treaty. It is, of course, fully understood that we will not agree to that. We see here a bypass route to securing military superiority.

I trust, Mr. President, you recall our discussion of this subject in Geneva. At that time I said that should the United States rush with weapons into space, we would not help it. We would do our utmost to devalue such efforts and make them futile. You may rest assured that we have every means to achieve this and, should the need arise, we shall use those means.

We favor the strengthening of the ABM Treaty regime. This is precisely the reason for our position that work should be confined to laboratories and that the Treaty should be strictly observed for a period of up to 15 years. Should this be the case, it would be possible – and this is our proposal – to agree to significant reductions of strategic offensive arms. We are prepared to do this without delay, and it would thereby be demonstrated in practice that neither side seeks military superiority.

Second. As far as medium-range missiles are concerned the Soviet Union has proposed an optimum solution – complete elimination of U.S. and Soviet missiles in Europe. We have also agreed to an interim option – and that, without taking into account the modernization of British and French nuclear systems.

Following our well-known steps towards accommodation, the issue of verification would seem no longer to be an obstacle. Yet, the U.S. side has now "discovered" another obstacle, namely, the Soviet medium range missiles in Asia. Nevertheless, I believe that here, as well, a mutually acceptable formula can be found and I am ready to propose one, provided there is certainty that a willingness to resolve the issue of medium-range missiles in Europe does exist.

Third. The attitude of the United States to the moratorium on nuclear testing is a matter of deep disappointment – and not only in the Soviet Union. The United States administration is making every effort to avoid this key problem, to subsume it in talk of other issues.

You are aware of my views in this regard: the attitude of a country to the cessation of nuclear testing is the touchstone of its policy in the field of disarmament and international security – and, indeed, in safeguarding peace in general.

Arguments to the effect that nuclear testing is needed to ensure reliability of nuclear arsenals are untenable. Today there are other methods to ensure this, without nuclear explosions. After all, the United

States does not test devices with yields in excess of 150-200 kilotons, although 70 per cent of the U.S. nuclear arsenal – and in our case the percentage is not smaller – consists of weapons with yields exceeding that threshold.

Modern science combined with a political willingness to agree to any adequate verification measures, including on-site inspections, ensure effective verification of the absence of nuclear explosions. So there too there is room for mutually acceptable solutions.

I have addressed specifically three questions which, in my opinion, are of greatest importance. They are the ones to which positive solutions are expected from the U.S.S.R. and the U.S.A. They are a matter of concern to the whole world, they are being discussed everywhere. Naturally, we are in favor of productive discussions of other major issues as well, such as reductions of armed forces and conventional armaments, a chemical weapons ban, regional problems, and humanitarian questions. Here too, common approaches and cooperation should be sought. Yet, the three questions mentioned above remain the key issues.

But in almost a year since Geneva there has been no movement on these issues. Upon reflection and after having given thought to your last letter I have come to the conclusions that the negotiations need a major impetus; otherwise they would continue to mark time while creating only the appearance of preparations for our meeting on American soil.

They will lead nowhere unless you and I intervene personally. I am convinced that we shall be able to find solutions, and I am prepared to discuss with you in a substantive way all possible approaches to them and identify such steps as would make it possible – after prompt follow-up by appropriate government agencies – to make my visit to the United States a really productive and fruitful one. This is exactly what the entire world is expecting from a second meeting between the leaders of the Soviet Union and the United States.

That is why an idea has come to my mind to suggest to you, Mr. President, that, in the very near future and setting aside all other matters, we have a quick one-on-one meeting, let us say in Iceland or in London, may be just for one day, to engage in a strictly confidential, private and frank discussion (possibly with only our foreign ministers present). The discussion – which would not be a detailed one, for its purpose and significance would be to demonstrate political will – would result in instructions to our respective agencies to draft agreements on two or three very specific questions, which you and I could sign during my visit to the United States

I look forward to your early reply.

Respectfully,

M. GORBACHEV

[On September 30, just two weeks after Gorbachev wrote the above letter, Reagan walked into the White House Press Room and announced that he and Gorbachev agreed to meet in Iceland, on October 11, for two days of talks to "prepare for the General Secretary's visit to the United States."

REYKJAVIK SUMMIT
OCTOBER 11-12, 1986

Reagan and Gorbachev met for the second time in Reykjavik, Iceland. Unlike their Geneva meeting the year before, at which Reagan and Gorbachev used their time to find ways to start to trust each other, thanks to their continued correspondence both Reagan and Gorbachev went to Reykjavik less guarded than at Geneva. The two leaders used the trust they had established to come closer to achieving their mutual goal of the complete elimination of nuclear weapons than at any previous time.

Although they failed to accomplish that ultimate goal, both Reagan and Gorbachev realized there was much they could agree on. For example, both thought a good starting point would be a fifty percent reduction in offensive ballistic missiles. Both also agreed that intermediate range nuclear forces capable of striking targets in Europe should be eliminated.

Of course disagreements remained. In terms of intermediate range weapons, Reagan thought it best for a global elimination of intermediate range weapons while Gorbachev was concerned that the Soviet Union would be vulnerable to China if it eliminated its intermediate range nuclear forces in Asia. The two though settled on a preliminary agreement for a complete elimination of intermediate range forces in the European theater and a limit of 100 intermediate range nuclear forces for both sides in Asia.

But the most significant disagreement to surface at Reykjavik, and one which would linger throughout the Reagan administration, involved whether or not the United States and Soviet Union would continue to adhere to the 1972 Anti-Ballistic Missile (ABM) Treaty. Under the ABM Treaty the United States and Soviet Union agreed to no more than 100 ground-based ballistic missile interceptors as well as restrictions on testing weapons in space. Reagan hoped Gorbachev would agree to modify the Treaty to accommodate space-based testing for SDI. Gorbachev could not have disagreed more. He told Reagan that his proposed modifications would essentially kill the ABM Treaty. Gorbachev argued it was better to strengthen the ABM Treaty, rather than weaken it, as Reagan proposed, by allowing space-based testing outside of laboratories.

CHAPTER THREE

SDI & INF

"There has to be an answer to all these questions because some day people are going to ask why we didn't do something now about getting rid of nuclear weapons."[12]

*"I have my own answer:
It is possible to proceed immediately with a 50 percent reduction."[13]*

"We do not want to be in the position of defending ourselves by saying that we have done nothing when we should have acted."[14]

---

[12] Reagan, speaking at the September 8, 1987 national security council meeting.

[13] Reagan to Gorbachev during their December 9, 1987 meeting in Washington discussing a proposal to reduce both countries nuclear weapons by 50 percent.

[14] Gorbachev to Reagan during their December 9, 1987 working lunch at the White House.

Reagan, on February 17, sent joint letters to Speaker of the House Wright and Senator Pell (Chairman of the Senate Foreign Relations Committee) transmitting a report on Compliance with Arms Control Agreements. The short cover letter noted:

> In previous reports to the Congress, the United States has made clear its concerns about Soviet noncompliance. These concerns remain. The United States Government takes equally seriously its own commitments to arms control agreements and sets rigid standards and procedures for assuring that it meets its obligations. The United States has been and remains in compliance with all current treaty obligations and political commitments.
>
> In view of the continued pattern of uncorrected Soviet violations and the increasing magnitude and threat of Soviet strategic forces, I decided on May 27, 1986, to end the U.S. policy of observing the SALT I Interim Agreement (which had expired, and which the Soviets were violating) and the SALT II Treaty (which was never ratified; which, had it been ratified, would have expired on December 31, 1985; and which the Soviets were violating). These agreements are now behind us, and Soviet allegations and the facts of Soviet compliance with regard to these agreements are therefore not discussed in this year's report. For our part, we will continue to exercise utmost restraint in our strategic force programs as we press for equitable and effectively verifiable agreements on deep reductions in U.S. and Soviet nuclear arsenals.

About three weeks later, on March 3, Reagan announced that a new round of arms control negotiations would soon begin with the Soviet Union. And a month later, Reagan sent Gorbachev a letter, dated April 10, reminding him that "it has been a long time since you and I last communicated directly. ... Together we can make the difference in the future course of world events. Let us pray that you and I can continue our dialogue so that the future will be one of peace and prosperity for both our nations and for the world."

That same day, April 10, Reagan was in Los Angeles and used the opportunity to give a major speech on U.S.-Soviet relations to a luncheon organized by the Los Angeles World Affairs Council. "From the very first days of this administration, I have insisted that our relations with the Soviets be based on realism rather than illusion," Reagan told the group. He then explained that he asked the Soviet Union "to join us in a mutual 50 percent cut in our strategic nuclear arsenals in a way that strengthens stability."

On April 16, after Secretary of State Shultz returned from talks in Moscow, Reagan told the press he was still "optimistic about an agreement this year." A few weeks later, the day before the next round of the Geneva arms control negotiations were set to begin, Reagan told the press corps he had "directed our U.S. START negotiator to intensify efforts to reach agreement on reducing strategic offensive nuclear arms by 50 percent." "I am firmly convinced that a START agreement is within our grasp, even this year, if the Soviets are prepared to resolve the remaining outstanding issues."

Soviet Foreign Minister Shevardnadze hand-delivered an eight-page letter on arms control from Gorbachev to Reagan on September 15. Gorbachev's letter acknowledged that an intermediate range nuclear forces treaty was "within reach," but an agreement still needed to be reached on verification and a global zero solution for intermediate range nuclear weapons. In terms of reaching an agreement on the ABM Treaty, Gorbachev wrote:

> Things are not as good with regard to working out agreement on the ABM Treaty regime, on preventing the extension of the arms race into space. Whereas we have submitted a constructive draft agreement that takes into account the U.S. attitude to the question of research on strategic defense, the U.S. side continues to take a rigid stand. However, without finding a mutually acceptable solution to the space problem it will be impossible to reach final agreement on radically reducing strategic offensive arms, which is what you and I spoke about in both Geneva and Reykjavik.

Reagan responded the next day with a short letter emphasizing that the Shevardnadze meeting was a constructive and useful step toward "our common search for peace."

April 10, 1987

Dear Mr. General Secretary:

It has been a long time since you and I last communicated directly. I am pleased that the visit of Secretary Shultz to Moscow offers us an opportunity to resume our direct dialogue.

I can recall at Geneva sitting before a fireplace and commenting that you and I were in a unique position. Together we can make the difference in the future course of world events. Let us pray that you and I can continue our dialogue so that the future will be one of peace and prosperity for both our nations and for the world.

I can also recall commenting to you that the very reason we are engaged in arms reductions negotiations is because of military competition that stems from the fundamental mistrust between our governments. If we are able to eliminate that distrust, arms reductions negotiations will be much easier.

There has been a recent incident that has caused problems between our two countries, and I feel strongly about this issue. At the same time, however, I am encouraged by many of the steps you are taking to modernize your own country and by the improved dialogue between us on arms reductions. There has also been some progress on human rights, although much more needs to be done. But the dialogue on regional issues has been quite fruitless so far, and I hope that we can make strenuous efforts in this area, especially on Afghanistan.

Secretary Shultz will come to Moscow prepared to deal with broad range of issues. He will carry with him positions that I have reviewed carefully and that are designed to improve the climate between our two countries and to build on the progress we have already made in the arms reductions area.

I look forward to positive discussions during Secretary Shultz's visit, and to a personal report from him immediately upon his return. Nancy joins me in sending very best regards to you and Raisa.

Sincerely,

Ronald Reagan

July 18, 1987

Dear Mr. President,

I have carefully read your message and considered the views contained in it.

We, too, are seriously concerned over the growing tensions in the Persian Gulf area. We discussed this issue more than once with the U.S. side, including at the time of Secretary of State Shultz's visit to Moscow. Our position of principle on this acute and complex problem has been set forth in the recent statement by the Soviet government.

One has to note with regret that thus far it has not been possible to slow down the dangerous trend in this region, let alone reverse it. There are several reasons for this.

First, it is the continuation of the senseless bloodshed between Iran and Iraq, which contributes, objectively, to aggravating the situation. Here, as I understand it, there are opportunities, and good ones, for joint actions by our two countries in the UN Security Council in favor of an earliest cessation of this prolonged conflict on just terms. There are, however, other sources of the escalation of tensions, which I shall discuss further.

Before doing so, I wish to inform you, Mr. President, about the many-sided efforts that the Soviet Union has been making to settle the Iran-Iraq conflict. As you may be aware, we have established special direct contacts with the leaderships of Iran and Iraq and are engaged at this time in intensive talks aimed at bringing the positions of the belligerents closer together, and encourage them toward a peaceful solution.

I would like to particularly emphasize that these efforts pursue no selfish ends, let alone directed against legitimate interests of third countries. Our only goal is to prevent a situation where a dangerous line would be crossed, beyond which a regional conflict could escalate into an international crisis, our objective is to help end the war.

We intend to continue and intensify those efforts.

Such an active bilateral diplomacy is called upon, as we see it, to organically supplement and bolster the broad multilateral efforts to end the Iran-Iraq war, and we attach paramount importance to our participation in those efforts. And I agree with your view that in this area the U.S. and the U.S.S.R. have good prospects for constructive cooperation. Currently, our two countries, along with other UN Security Council members, are playing an active role in working out effective measures to promptly channel the Iran-Iraq conflict toward peaceful solutions. Our representatives have been instructed to press on with the efforts seeking, in particular an immediate ceasefire, an end to all hostilities and a prompt withdrawal of all troops to internationally recognized borders.

It is our firm conviction that a special role in carrying out the decisions now being prepared by the world community belongs to the UN Secretary General. Indeed, it is on his actions that will depend no small degree the further steps which may be required if the adopted resolution is resisted by either of the parties in the conflict. In the event of such an undesirable development the recommendations of the Secretary General will, understandably, carry a lot of weight. In this connection, we expect, Mr. President, that you will find it possible to give necessary support to the peacemaking mission of the Secretary General and will join us in contributing to its success.

As for your proposal that experts participate in the work being done in the Security Council, I can reaffirm our positive attitude to it, given, naturally, the concurrence of the Council's other permanent members.

Now I must come back to the question of the causes for the increased tensions in the Persian Gulf area. I must say frankly: these are not confined to the continued hostilities between Iran and Iraq. We cannot ignore the buildup of the U.S. military presence in the area, to say nothing of the contrived pretexts used in an attempt to disguise it. True, there are not only your warships, but ours as well in the Persian Gulf. However, simply looking at the facts as they are – and I am sure you have every possibility to do so – would show that our naval presence is in no way comparable to yours either in scale or in operational functions. A few Soviet warships to which references are being made in Washington, are escorting on a temporary basis our merchant vessels at the request and with the knowledge of the littoral states.

Moreover, guided by the desire to use every opportunity to make the situation better, the Soviet Government has proposed that all warships of the states outside of the region be withdrawn as early as possible while Iran and Iraq in their turn refrain from actions which would pose a threat to international shipping.

We are gratified by the constructive reaction of most countries, including those involved in the conflict, to that proposal. We would like to expect that the US leadership will also view it in a positive light, in the spirit of cooperation.

Also, some statements by representatives of your administration seem to indicate an interest on the American side. If such an impression is justified, then we would be prepared to discuss this question with the US in more concrete terms in any format suitable for you.

Speaking in broader terms, I want to emphasize that I share the idea which you expressed in concluding your letter: when our countries decide to act together, the results will not be long in coming.

Sincerely,

M. GORBACHEV

September 15, 1987

Dear Mr. President,

I think you and I were right when last October we arrived at what was virtually a concurring view that our meeting in Reykjavik had been an important landmark along the path towards specific and urgently needed measures to genuinely reduce nuclear arms. Over the past several months the Soviet Union and the United States have made substantial headway in that direction. Today, our two countries stand on the threshold of an important agreement which would bring about – for the first time in history – an actual reduction in nuclear arsenals. Nuclear disarmament being the exceptionally complex matter that it is, the important thing is to take a first step, to clear the psychological barrier which stands between the deeply rooted idea that security hinges on nuclear weapons and on objective perception of the realities of the nuclear world. Then the conclusion is inevitable that genuine security can only be achieved through real disarmament.

We have come very close to the point, and the question now is whether we will take that first step which the peoples of the world are so eagerly awaiting. This is precisely what I would like to discuss at greater length in this letter being fully aware that not too much time remains for the preparation of the agreement between us. The Reykjavik understandings give us a chance to reach agreement. We are facing the dilemma of either rapidly completing an agreement on intermediate and shorter-range missiles or missing the chance to reach an accord, which, as a result of joint efforts has almost entirely taken shape.

It would probably be superfluous to say that the Soviet Union prefers the first option. In addition to our basic commitment to the goal of abolishing nuclear weapons, which is the point of departure for our policy, we also proceed from the belief that at this juncture of time there appears to be a convergence of the lines of interests of the United States, the Soviet Union, Europe, and the rest of the world. If we fail to take advantage of such a favorable confluence of circumstances, those lines will diverge, and who knows when they might converge again. Then we would risk losing time and momentum, with the inevitable consequences of the further militarization of the Earth and the extension of the arms race into space. In this context I agree with the thought you expressed that "the opportunity before us is too great to let pass by."

To use an American phrase, the Soviet Union has gone its mile towards a fair agreement, and even more than a mile. Of course, I am far from asserting that the U.S. side has done nothing to advance the work on intermediate and shorter-range missiles. We could not have come to the point where the treaty is within reach had the United States not made steps in our direction. And yet, there is still no answer to the question why Washington has hardened its stance in upholding a number of positions which are clearly one-sided and, I would say, contrived. I would ask you once again to weigh carefully all the factors involved and convey to me your final decision on whether the agreement is to be concluded now or postponed, or even set aside. It is time you and I took a firm stand on this matter.

I further request that you give careful thought to the recent important evolution in our positions on intermediate and shorter-range missiles, which in effect assures accord. We are ready to conclude an agreement under which neither the United States nor the Soviet Union would have any missiles in those categories.

The implementation of such a decision would be subject to strict reciprocal verification, including, of course, on-site inspections of both the process of the missiles' destruction and the cessation of their production.

I have to say that we are proposing to you a solution which in important aspects is virtually identical with the proposals that were, at various points, put forward by the U.S. side. For that reason in particular, there should be no barriers to reaching an agreement, and the artificial obstacles erected by the U.S. delegation should naturally disappear, which, as I understand, will be facilitated by the decision of the F.R.G. government not to modernize the West German Pershing 1A missiles and to eliminate them. Of course, we have no intention to interfere in U.S. alliance relations, including those with the F.R.G. However, the question of what happens to the U.S. warheads intended for the West German missiles needs to be clarified.

We are proposing fair and equitable terms for an agreement. Let me say very candidly and without diplomatic niceties: we have in effect opened up the reserves of our positions in order to facilitate an agreement. Out position is clear and honest: we call for the total elimination of an entire class of missiles with ranges between 500 and 5,500 kilometers and of all warheads for those missiles. The fate of an agreement on intermediate and shorter-range missiles now depends entirely on the U.S. leadership and on your personal willingness, Mr. President, to conclude a deal. As for our approach, it will be constructive, you can count on that.

If we assume that the U.S. side, proceeding from considerations of equivalent security, will go ahead with the conclusion of the treaty – and this is what we hope is going to happen – then there is no doubt that this will impart a strong impetus to bringing our positions closer together in a very real way on other questions in the nuclear and space area, which are even more important for the security of the U.S.S.R. and the U.S.A. and with which you and have come to grips after Reykjavik.

What I have in mind specifically are the issues of strategic offensive arms and space. Those are the key issues of security, and our stake in reaching agreement on them is certainly not at all diminished by the fact that we have made headway on intermediate and short-range missiles. What is more, it is this area that is pivotal to the U.S.-Soviet strategic relationship, and hence to the entire course of military-strategic developments in the world.

At the negotiations in Geneva on those questions the delegations, as you know, have started drafting an agreed text of a treaty on strategic offensive arms. The Soviet side is seeking to speed up, to the maximum possible extent, progress in this work and shows its readiness to accommodate the other side and to seek compromise solutions. To reach agreement, however, a reciprocal readiness for compromise is, of course, required on the part of the United States.

Things are not as good with regard to working out agreement on the ABM Treaty regime, on preventing the extension of the arms race into space. Whereas we have submitted a constructive draft agreement that takes into account the U.S. attitude to the question of research on strategic defense, the U.S. side continues to take a rigid stand. However, without finding a mutually acceptable solution to the space problem it will be impossible to reach final agreement on radically reducing strategic offensive arms, which is what you and I spoke about in both Geneva and Reykjavik.

If we are to be guided by a desire to find a fair solution to both these organically interrelated problems, issues relating to space can be resolved. The Soviet Union is ready to make additional efforts to that end. But it is clear that this cannot be done through our efforts alone, if attempts to secure unilateral advantages are not abandoned.

I propose, Mr. President, that necessary steps be taken, in Geneva and through other channels, particularly at a high level, in order to speed up the pace of negotiations so that full-scale agreement could be reached within the new few months both on the radical reduction of strategic offensive arms and on emerging strict observance of the ABM Treaty.

If all these efforts were crowned with success we would be able to provide a firm basis for a stable and forward-moving development not just of the Soviet-U.S. relationship but of international relations as a whole for many years ahead. We would leave behind what was, frankly, a complicated stretch in world politics, and you and I would crown in a befitting manner the process of interaction of the central issues of security which began in Geneva.

I think that both of us should not lose sight of other important security issues, where fairly good prospects have not emerged of cooperating for the sake of reaching agreement.

I would like to single out in particular the question of the real opportunities that have appeared for solving at last the problem of the complete elimination of chemical weapons globally. Granted that the preparation of a convention banning chemical weapons depends not only on the efforts of our two countries, still it is the degree of agreement between our positions that in effect predetermines progress in this matter. It is our common duty to bring this extremely important process to fruition.

If the veneer of polemics is removed from the problem of reducing conventional arms, a common interest will be evident in this area too. This is the interest of stability at a lower level of arms, which can be achieved through substantial reductions in armed forces and armaments, through removing the existing asymmetries and imbalances. Accordingly, we have fairly good prospects of working together to draw up a mutually acceptable *mandate for negotiations on conventional arms. The Vienna meeting would thus become a major stage in terms of a military dimension, in addition to the economic, human and other dimensions.*

One more consideration: we believe that the time has come to remove the cloak of dangerous secrecy from the military doctrines of the two alliances, of the U.S.S.R. and the U.S.A. In this process of giving greater transparency to our military guidelines, meetings of military officials at the highest level could also play a useful role.

Does it not seem paradoxical to you, Mr. President, that we have been able to bring our positions substantially closer together in an area where the nerve knots of our security are located and yet we have been unable so far to find a common language on another important aspect, namely, regional conflicts? Not only do they exacerbate the international situation, they often bring our relations to a pitch of high tension. In the meantime, in the regions concerns – whether in Asia, which is increasingly moving to the forefront of international politics, the Near East or Central America – encouraging changes are now under way, reflecting a search for a peaceful settlement. I have in mind, in particular, the growing desire for national reconciliation. This should be given careful attention and, I believe, encouragement and support.

As you can see, the Soviet leadership once again reaffirms its strong intention to build Soviet-U.S. relations in a constructive and businesslike spirit. Time may flow particularly fast for those relations, and we should treat it as something extremely precious. We are in favor of making full use of Eduard Shevardnadze's visit to Washington to find practical solutions to key problems. In the current situation this visit assumes increased importance. Our foreign minister is ready for detailed discussions with U.S. leaders on all questions, including ways of reaching agreement on problems under discussion in Geneva and the prospects and possible options for developing contacts at the summit level. He has all the necessary authority with regard to that.

I want to emphasize that, as before, I am personally in favor of actively pursing a businesslike and constructive dialogue with you.

Sincerely,

M. GORBACHEV

September 16, 1987

Dear Mr. General Secretary:

It was a great pleasure for me to receive personal greetings from you and Mrs. Gorbachev yesterday. Nancy and I appreciate your thoughtfulness.

At the signing of the Agreement on Nuclear Risk Reductions Centers, I said that I look forward to the day when you and I can come together to sign even more historic agreements in our common search for peace. My meeting yesterday with Foreign Minister Shevardnadze and his delegation was a constructive and useful step in that direction.

Nancy and I wish to take this opportunity to convey to you and Mrs. Gorbachev our personal best wishes and our hope that the coming months will see further steps toward our common goals.

Sincerely,

Ronald Reagan

THE WASHINGTON SUMMIT
DECEMBER 7-10, 1987

By the time Gorbachev flew to Washington for their third one-on-one meeting, the terms of an agreement to eliminate all intermediate range nuclear forces had been agreed upon. All that was left was for Reagan and Gorbachev to sign the official documents outlining the terms of the Intermediate-Range Nuclear Forces (INF) Treaty.

The signing of the INF Treaty, one of the first official acts Gorbachev did in Washington, was an historic event. The Treaty marked the first time an entire class of nuclear weapons was eliminated. It also marked a recognition among the Soviet and American leaders that possession of intermediate range nuclear forces, with their short flight time and, in the case of the Soviet Union, mobile launching pads, posed an unnecessary risk to Soviet, American, European, and actually all human life.

The INF Treaty, however, only required each side to reduce their nuclear forces by about four percent. In real numbers that meant that the United States and Soviet Union still had around 30,000 active nuclear weapons even after all the intermediate range nuclear forces were eliminated.

With the INF Treaty out of the way, Gorbachev and Reagan were able to use the rest of their time together in Washington to discuss ways to reduce their strategic arms, known as the START negotiations. The START negotiations continued from the Reykjavik Summit, the year before, during which Reagan and Gorbachev agreed in principle to at least a fifty percent reduction in offensive ballistic missiles. The hold up at Reykjavik, as it would be in Washington, was Reagan's insistence that the United States be able to conduct space-based testing for defensive weapons outside of laboratories. Gorbachev could not agree, again claiming that doing so would violate that ABM Treaty and lead to an arms race in space.

Despite the lack of progress towards a START Treaty, Gorbachev would leave Washington hopeful that an agreement could be reached before Reagan visited Moscow in May. "I will soon be saying goodbye," Gorbachev told Reagan in their last one-on-one in Washington.

> I have arrived at the conclusion that this third summit has been a landmark. It has witnessed important agreements and other questions had been discussed intensively. Most importantly, the atmosphere has been good. There have also been more elements of mutual understanding, and I would like to acknowledge President Reagan's efforts towards making this a successful summit, as well as to the contributions of other American participants.

> I would like the momentum achieved at the Summit to continue. On my way to lunch today at the White House I rode with Vice President Bush. We had looked out of the car and seen Americans responding warmly to what happened in the negotiations. When the car stopped at a red light, I jumped out and had had a spontaneous conversation with some passerby. When it was time to go, I did not want to leave the conversation.

Reagan agreed. "The General Secretary and I have the right to feel good about the Summit," the president reflected. "When we first met in Geneva, I told you, Mr. General Secretary, that ours was a unique situation. We represented two countries that could initiate another world war. Or, we could make sure that there would not be another world war." Although the two leaders were successful in preventing another world war, when Reagan traveled to Moscow in May 1988, they had yet to agree on another historic arms control treaty.

CHAPTER FOUR

GOING FOR THE GOLD

"I want to leave as a legacy as complete and coherent an arms reduction position as I can."[15]

"It is our impression that we have to tango alone, as if our partner has taken a break."[16]

---

[15] President Reagan to his NSC advisors. May 23, 1988.

[16] Gorbachev in a letter to Reagan. September 20, 1988.

SECRETARY OF STATE SHULTZ, White House National Security Adviser Colin Powell, and Special Assistant to the President for Arms Control Paul Nitze, flew to Moscow in February for discussions on reaching a START agreement. Shultz and Gorbachev agreed that they were "determined" to get a document ready to be signed in May during Reagan's official visit.

Gorbachev, however, was skeptical about American intentions. "Once the Soviet side has accepted a U.S. proposal," Gorbachev told Shultz, "the U.S. side takes it back. This is becoming routine."

Back in Washington, Reagan instructed his staff to "work for the gold," which meant finding a way to reach a START agreement. But Reagan and Gorbachev had different priorities. Gorbachev focused on how to reach an agreement that included restricting space-based testing for the Strategic Defense Initiative. Reagan, as he had time and time again, instructed his staff that no agreement would be possible if it included restrictions on space-based testing.

Gorbachev was right to be skeptical. Although Reagan seemed to have hoped that he would be flying to Moscow to sign another historic arms reductions treaty, he would not do so if Gorbachev still insisted on tying a START agreement to restrictions on space-based testing. Although Gorbachev may have budged, as he did in 1991, in 1988 it seems that other issues, like verification, also stood in the way of another arms reductions treaty. In all likelihood, Reagan and those around him were just not prepared to take the next step towards the elimination of nuclear weapons.

Despite the lack of another arms agreement, the Moscow Summit, marking the fourth meeting between Reagan and Gorbachev in less than three years, succeeded thanks to lessened expectations. Reagan focused on human rights, and spent his time visiting the historic Moscow sights. Gorbachev, realizing an arms agreement would not be reached, focused on moving forward. Most importantly, Reagan essentially acknowledged that the Cold War was over when he told reports while standing in Red Square that he no longer considered the Soviet Union an evil empire.

Although Reagan and Gorbachev failed to accomplish the complete elimination of nuclear weapons, they did something perhaps more important: they gave the peoples of the United States and Soviet Union hope that their two nations could peacefully coexist.

THE MOSCOW SUMMIT
MAY 29-31, 1988

Reagan started his first private meeting in Moscow by handing Gorbachev a list of a dozen or so names of people living in the Soviet Union that had trouble emigrating. Reagan told Gorbachev that these names were "brought to my personal attention, by relatives and friends." In accepting the list, Gorbachev reminded Reagan that in terms of access to education, employment and health care, Blacks and Hispanics in the United States are far behind Whites, and even though there are lower living conditions in the Soviet Union than in the United States, the socio-economic gap is not as large as it is in the United States.

REAGAN: I wish to take up another topic that has been a kind of personal dream of mine. I have been reluctant to raise it with you, but I am going to do it now anyway. If word got out that this was even being discussed, I would deny I said anything about it.

I am suggesting this because we are friends, and you can do something of benefit not only to yourself, but to the image of your country worldwide. The Soviet Union had a church – in a recent speech you liberalized some of the rules – the Orthodox Church for example. Would it be possible for you to rule that religion is part of the peoples' rights, that people of any religion – whether Islam with its mosque, the Jewish faith, Protestants or the Ukrainian church – could go to the church of their choice.

In the United States, under our constitution, there is complete separation of church and state. People endured a long sea voyage to a primitive land to worship as they pleased. What I have suggested could go a long way to solving the Soviet emigration problem. Potential emigrants often want to leave because of their limited ability to worship the God they believe in.

GORBACHEV: The problem of religion in the Soviet Union is not a serious one. There are not big problems with freedom of worship. I was baptized, though I am now a non-believer, which reflects a certain evolution of Soviet society. All are free to believe or not believe in God. That is a person's freedom. The U.S. side is actively for freedom, but why is it then that non-believers in the U.S. sometimes feel suppressed? Why do non- believers not have the same rights as believers?

REAGAN: They do. I have a son who is an atheist, though he calls himself an agnostic.

GORBACHEV: Why are atheists criticized in the United States? This means a certain infringement of their freedom. It means there is a limitation on their freedom. I read the U.S. newspapers – there should be free choice to believe or not to believe in God.

REAGAN: This is also true for people in the United States. Religion could not be taught in the public schools. When we said freedom, that means the government has nothing to do with it. There are people who spend considerable money to build and maintain schools that are religious. I heard that you recently lifted restrictions on such contributions. There are people volunteering to restore churches. In my country the government cannot prevent that, but cannot help either. Tax money cannot be spent to help churches. It is true that there are private schools with the same courses as public schools but with religious education – this is because there are people willing to pay to create and support them. But in public schools supported by taxes, you cannot even say a prayer.

GORBACHEV: After the revolution, there were excesses in that sphere. As in any revolution, there were certain excesses, and not only in that sphere but in others as well. But today the trend is precisely in the direction you mentioned. There has been conflicts between the authorities and religious activists, but only when they were anti-Soviet, and there have been fewer such conflicts recently. I am sure they will disappear.

When we speak of perestroika, that meant change, a democratic expansion of democratic procedures, of rights, of making them real – and that referred to religion, too.

REAGAN: Can we take a look at religious rights under the U.S. Constitution? There are some people – not many, but some – who are against war. They are allowed to declare themselves conscientious objectors, when they can prove that their objection is a matter of faith not to take up arms even to defend their country. They can be put in uniform doing non-violent jobs – they could not escape from service – but they could not be made to kill against their religion. In every war there are a few such people, and sometimes they perform heroic deeds in the service of others. They can refuse to bear arms.

If you can see clear to do what I asked – ruling that religious freedom was a right – I feel very strongly that you would be a hero and that much of the feeling against your country would disappear like water in hot sun. If there is anyone in this room who later said I have given such advice, I will call the person a liar and say that I never said that. This is not something to be negotiated, not something someone should be told to do.

I have a letter from the widow of a young World War II soldier. He was lying in a shell hole at midnight, awaiting an order to attack. He had never been a believer, because he had been told God did not exist. But as he looked up at the stars he voiced a prayer hoping that, if he died in battle, God would accept him. That piece of paper was found on the body of a young Russian soldier who was killed in that battle.

GORBACHEV: Mr. President, I still feel that you do not have the full picture concerning freedom of religion in the Soviet Union. We not only have many nationalities and ethnic groups, but many religious denominations – Orthodox, Catholic, Muslim, various denominations of Protestants, like the Baptists – and they practice their religion on a very large scale. You are going to meet the

Patriarch and visit monasteries. If you ask the
Patriarch, he will tell you about the religious
situation in the Soviet Union.

With their wives waiting and time running out, Reagan and Gorbachev
agreed to break protocol (at least in private) and call each other "Ron" and
"Mikhail". But before the two joined their wives, Reagan wanted to tell one
more story:

REAGAN: There was one thing I've long yearned to
do for my atheist son – I've long to serve him the
perfect gourmet dinner, to have him enjoy the
meal, and then to ask if he believed there was a
cook. I've wondered how he would answer.

GORBACHEV: The only answer possible is yes.

Reagan and Gorbachev continued to meet over the next few days. With
no significant arms control agreements on the table, Reagan used his time
with Gorbachev to continue to push for increased human rights and
religious freedom reforms in the Soviet Union. Publically, the President
and First Lady also pressed the human rights issue by visiting monasteries
and meeting with Soviet refuseniks, dissidents, and other human rights
cases.

At Moscow State University, "looking ahead to the future of the
relationship and the challenges of the modern world," Reagan told the
Soviet students and faculty:

"We do not know what the conclusion will be of this journey, but we're
hopeful that the promise of reform will be fulfilled. In this Moscow spring,
this May 1988, we may be allowed that hope: that freedom, like the fresh
green sapling planted over Tolstoy's grave, will blossom forth at last in the
rich fertile soil of your people and culture."

A few more meetings with Gorbachev followed, and on the final night
of the Summit, the President and First Lady were the honored guests of the
Gorbachev's at the Bolshoi ballet. Dinner followed at the Gorbachev's
private Dacha outside Moscow, and the next morning was spent quickly
thanking everyone for their help: a stop at the Embassy at 9 A.M.; the
Gorbachev's at 10 A.M.; the official departure ceremony at 10:45 A.M.; and
then an 11:00 A.M. lift off to London where the Reagan's had a 5:15 P.M.
date for tea with Queen Elizabeth II. Tea was followed by a 6:15 P.M. one-
on-one with Prime Minister Thatcher, and then a 7:30 P.M. dinner with
members of the British Parliament.

On the tenth and last day of the trip, Reagan spent an hour in the morning with Japanese Prime Minister Takeshita, and then spoke at Guildhall about how the causes of peace and freedom still bring Britain and the United States together. Reagan referred to his trip as "quite possibly... a new era in history, a time of lasting change in the Soviet Union."

[Reagan and Gorbachev exchanged several letters following the Moscow Summit. Both leaders knew, however, that their correspondence would shortly be coming to a close, as Americans would soon elect a new president.

The following letters, dated June 23, September 13, and September 20, represent some of the final letters between Reagan and Gorbachev. The missing letters, unfortunately, could not be located. The chapter closes with the final meeting between President Reagan and General Secretary Gorbachev, on Governor's Island, New York.

That November, Americans soundly elected Reagan's Vice-President, George H. W. Bush, as their 41st president. Bush defeated Massachusetts Governor Michael Dukakis in large part thanks to the goodwill Reagan gained among Americans due to improved U.S.-Soviet relations.

President-Elect Bush joined Reagan and Gorbachev at their final meeting. The president-elect, however, saw his role as more of an observer. He was there to greet the soviet general secretary, but not ready to discuss any issues of substance. In fact, Bush, who had always been skeptical of Reagan's efforts to improve U.S.-Soviet relations, would soon announce a freeze of all U.S.-Soviet negotiations until he had sufficient time to review the negotiating records.]

June 23, 1988

Dear Mr. President,

I see your letter as confirmation of the importance of the relationship between us, as evidence of your good feelings. Indeed, along with significant political results, our meeting in Moscow has been given an encouraging human dimension – not only in terms of our personal liking for each other, but also in terms of warmer relationship between our peoples and their more correct perception of each other.

The importance of all this transcends even the US-Soviet dialogue, whose regularity and pithiness are highly appreciated by our allies and the world community at large.

Raisa Maximovna and I have warm recollections of the hours that we spent in an open and spontaneous give-and-take with Mrs. Reagan and yourself. We are very please that you had an opportunity to see our people, speak with them, feel their sentiments and see that they sincerely want to build relations with America in the spirit of friendship, understanding and cooperation. The Soviet people, in turn, have met you up close and have come to appreciate your good will, and your role in everything that has been accomplished by our two countries together.

We are sending you a photo album. May it remind you and your wife of the remarkable days you spent in the Soviet union, days that are destined to be part of history.

With our best wishes to Mrs. Nancy Reagan and yourself.
                    Sincerely,
                    M. GORBACHEV

September 13, 1988

Dear Mr. President,

I have read your letter of August 12 very carefully.

I would like, in the frank and constructive spirit that characterizes our dialogue, to share with you my thoughts regarding the question of AMB Treaty compliance raised in your letter.

This question has been repeatedly discussed both by ourselves and by our experts, most recently during the latest consultations to review the ABM Treaty. In the course of the negotiations the sides have stated their concerns regarding compliance with the treaty. Regrettably, thus far the US representatives have failed to provide persuasive answers to the questions we raised, while the Soviet side has clarified in great detail the situation surrounding the radar which was under construction in the Krasnoyarsk area, having reiterated that it is not a missile attack warning radar. In light of our answers the complaints expressed again and again by the US side cause perplexity and suggest that, perhaps, there are some other, more far-reaching calculations behind them.

I think you will agree with me that it would be impardonable if our mutual complaints about the violations of the ABM Treaty were to undermine all that we, thanks to the efforts of both sides, have succeeded in accomplishing to improve US-Soviet relations. With the aim of allowing this occur we have, as a gesture of good will, not only discontinued the construction of the Krasnoyarsk radar, but have also expressed willingness to dismantle its equipment, if our countries reach agreement to observe the ABM Treaty as signed in 1972. Such a solution would represent a true confirmation of the commitment of the sides of the ABM Treaty, a commitment about which you, Mr. President, have repeatedly spoken and written to me.

At the same time I cannot fail to emphasize that we are increasingly concerned over the situation that has arisen in connection with the construction of US radars in Thule and Flyingdales Moor. In the assessment of our experts, the now operational Thule radar is a clear violation of the ABM Treaty. Your specialists deny that. But, as you know, an American proverb says: "Seeing is believing". So we are hoping that you will agree to a visit of this radar by Soviet specialists.

As for the Krasnoyarsk radar, I wish to inform you of our decision which will once and for all put an end to all speculations about its nature, to wit: we are ready to establish on the base of this radar a center for international cooperation in the interest of the peaceful use of outer space. This center could be incorporated into the system of a World Space Organization which we proposed, so as to make it possible for all states to participate in the peaceful exploration and use of outer space.

We are prepared to discuss with United States' representatives, as well as with other interested countries, the concrete measures that would make it possible to transform the Krasnoyarsk radar into a Center for International Cooperation in Peaceful Space Activities. I would like, through your intermediary, to invite American scientists to visit the Krasnoyarsk radar in order to discuss the questions connected therewith.

In conclusion, I wish to express my hope that your administration, Mr. President, will be guided in its practical actions by the desire to preserve the ABM Treaty as an important instrument for maintaining strategic stability in conditions where our two countries – I believe the agreement on that is not far away – will be implementing the 50 percent reduction in their strategic offensive arms. In this context, we will expect the US side also to take practical steps which would remove our concern over the US radars in Greenland and Great Britain.

Respectfully,
M. GORBACHEV

September 20, 1988

Dear Mr. President,

I take advantage of the visit of by Minister of Foreign Affairs Eduard A. Shevardnadze to Washington in order to continue our private discussion.

In one of our conversations in Moscow it was suggested that we might have a chance to meet once again this year to sign a treaty on drastic reductions in strategic offensive arms in the context of compliance with the ABM Treaty. Regrettably, this goal that both of us share has been set back in time, although I continue to think that it can still be attained, even if beyond this year.

I take some consolation in the awareness that still in effect is our agreement to do the utmost in the remaining months of your presidency to ensure the continuity and consistency of the fundamental course that we have chosen. As I recall, you said you would do your best to preserve the constructive spirit of dialogue, and I replied that in that respect our intentions were quite identical. And so they are indeed, which is a source of great hope for our two peoples.

Four months have gone by since the summit talks in Moscow – a short period of time given the dynamic and profound development in international affairs and those that fill the political calendar in the Soviet Union and the United States. Still, a great deal has been accomplished in putting into effect the jointly agreed platform for the further advancement of Soviet-US relations. For the first time in history, nuclear missiles have been destroyed, and unprecedented mutual verification of the just been process of nuclear disarmament is becoming an established and routine practice. In several regions of the world, a process of political settlement of conflicts and national reconciliation has got under way. The human dimension of our relations, to which we have agreed to give special attention, is becoming richer. Ordinary Soviet people continue to discover America for themselves, marching across it on a peace walk, and right now, as you are reading this letter, another public meeting between Soviet and US citizens is being held in Tbilisi.

Someone might object that in the past, say in the 1930s or 1970s, Soviet-US relations also had their upturns. I would think, however, that the current stage in our interaction is distinguished by several significant features. The four summit meetings over the past three years have laid good groundwork for our dialogue and raised it to a qualitatively new level. And, as we know, from high ground it is easier to see the path we have covered, the problems of the day, and the prospects that emerge.

A unique arrangement for practical interaction has been established, which is supported by fundamental political affirmations and, at the same time, filled with tangible content. This has been facilitated by the principal approach on which we have agreed already in Geneva, ie.. realism, a clear awareness of the essence of our differences, and a focus on active search for possible areas where our national interests may coincide. Thus, we gave ourselves a serious intellectual challenge – to view our differences and diversity not as a reason for permanent confrontation but as a motivation for intensive dialogue, mutual appreciation and enrichment.

Overall, we have been able to achieve fairly good results, to start a transition from confrontation to a policy of accommodation. And this is, probably, not just a result of a frank and constructive personal relationship, although, obviously, personal rapport is not the least important thin in politics. Paraphrasing a favorite phrase of yours, I would say that talking to each other people learn more about each other.

And yet, the main thing that made our common new policy a success is, above all, the fact that it reflects a gradually emerging balance of national interests, which we have been able in some measure to implement. We feel, in particular, that it is favorable to the development of new approaches, of new political thinking, first of all in our two countries – but also elsewhere. The experience of even the past few months indicates that an increasing number of third countries are beginning to readjust to our positive interaction, associating with it their interests and policies.

Ironically as it may sound, it is our view that the strength of what we have been able to accomplish owes quite a lot to how hard it was to do.

It is probably not by a mere chance that the jointly devised general course in the development of Soviet-US relations is now enjoying broad-based support in our two countries. So far as we know, both of your possible successors support, among other things, the key objective of concluding a treaty on 50 percent cutbacks in Soviet and US strategic arsenals. In the Soviet leadership, too, there is a consensus on this.

And yet it has not been possible to bring the Geneva negotiations to fruition, a fact about which I feel some unhappiness. It is our impression that we have to tango alone, as if our partner has taken a break.

In another letter to you, I have already addressed the matter which you raised in your letter of August 12 regarding compliance with the ABM Treaty. I think you would agree with me that it would be unforgiveable if our mutual complaints of violations of the ABM Treaty resulted in undermining what we have been able to accomplish to rectify Soviet-US relations through the efforts of both sides.

I would like Eduard Shevardnadze's visit to the United States and his talks with you and Secretary Shultz to result in reviving truly joint efforts to achieve deep cuts in strategic offensive arms. Our Minister has the authority to seek rapid progress on the basis of reciprocity in this exceptionally important area.

Today, the process of nuclear disarmament is objectively interrelated with the issues of deep reductions, and the elimination of asymmetries and imbalances, in conventional arms and complete prohibition of chemical weapons. In these areas too, there is a good chance of making headway toward agreements.

I am confident, Mr. President, that you and I can make a further contribution to the emerging process of settlement of regional conflicts, particularly to a consistent and honest compliance with the first accords that have already been concluded there.

In Moscow we also reinforced the foundation for a dynamic development of our bilateral relations and helped to open up new channels for communication between Soviet and American people, including your people and artists. All these good endeavors should be given practical effect, and we stand ready to do so. I am aware of your deep personal interest in questions of human rights. For me, too, it is a priority issue. We seem to have agreed that these problems require an in-depth consideration and a clear understanding of the true situation in both the United States and the Soviet Union. Traffic along this two-way street has begun and I hope that it will be intense.

Our relationship is a dynamic stream and you and I are working together to widen it. The stream cannot be slowed down, it can only be blocked or diverted. But that would not be in our interest.

Politics, of course, is the art of the possible, but it is only by working and maintaining a dynamic dialogue that we will put into effect what we have made possible, and will make possible tomorrow what is yet impossible today.

Sincerely,
Mikhail Gorbachev

REAGAN-GORBACHEV MEETING
GOVERNORS ISLAND, NEW YORK
DECEMBER 7, 1988

Reagan sent to Congress, on December 2, 1988, the Annual Report on Soviet Noncompliance with Arms Control Agreements. "This year's report reaffirms our 1987 findings of Soviet violations or probable violation of the ABM Treaty," the four-paragraph press statement noted. The report continued:

> We are particularly concerned about the Krasnoyarsk Radar, which is a significant violation of a central element of the ABM Treaty. We have made clear to the Soviets that their failure to correct this violation by dismantling the Radar in a verifiable manner that meets our criteria casts a shadow over the arms control process. We cannot conclude new strategic arms control agreements while this violation remains uncorrected. We also reserve all our rights under international law to take appropriate and proportionate responses, including the possibility of declaring a material breach.

We have discussed these violations repeatedly with the Soviet Union and have given them every opportunity to meet our concerns. If the Soviet Union is genuinely interested in a more constructive and stable long-term relationship, it will take the necessary steps to correct its violations.

A day latter Reagan used his weekly radio address to review the state of U.S.-Soviet relations.

My fellow Americans....This will be our last such meeting, and I must admit that I would not have predicted after first taking office that someday I would be waxing nostalgic about my meetings with Soviet leaders. But here we are for the fifth time, Mr. Gorbachev and I together, in the hope of furthering peace.

And always in my mind, I go back to that first summit held in 1985 at a private villa on the shores of Lake Geneva. At the first of our fireside talks, I said to Mr. Gorbachev that ours was a unique meeting between two people who had the power to start World War III or to begin a new era for humanity. The opportunity for such a new era is there and very real.

In his speech at the United Nations, directly before his meeting with Reagan and President-Elect George H.W. Bush, Gorbachev announced that the Soviet Union would begin unilateral disarmament actions by reducing conventional forces by 500,000, and removing thousands of tanks and tens of thousands of troops from Eastern Europe. The unilateral Soviet cuts, apparently, caught many in the U.S. by surprise, and as the memorandum of conversation between Reagan, Bush and Gorbachev show, Reagan and Bush barely acknowledged the Soviet announcement.

SUMMARY

GORBACHEV: I hope that what I said at the UN did not contain any surprises. I had wanted to address the logical construction of what had been done in recent years, as a matter of real policy. This is our fifth meeting. It is not a negotiating session, but at the same time it is our fifth meeting, and it is special, taking place as it does in this group.

REAGAN: It is a pleasure for me to commemorate our meetings. I well remember standing in front of the house before the lake in Geneva, waiting for you

	for that first meeting. Most of my people thought at the time it would be our only meeting.
GORBACHEV:	It is true that we have much to remember, and much to look forward to as well. This is true not just in a personal sense. The most important thing we have done is begin a movement in the right direction. Vice President Bush is here listening, but probably thinking to himself, "let them talk."
MEDIA:	Mr. Gorbachev, why did you announce troop cuts during your UN speech?
GORBACHEV:	As I just told the President and Vice President, what I announced was a continuation and implementation of what I first outlined on January 15, 1986.
	I appreciate what the President and I have accomplished in recent years. We have made a joint analysis, undertaken joint efforts, and taken real, specific steps forward. Today, at the UN, I outlined certain additional ideas that demonstrated the realistic nature of the policy and added to it. This was an invitation to work together, and not just to the U.S. What I said was grounded in common sense and experience.
MEDIA:	Mr. Gorbachev, do you expect the NATO allies, including the U.S., to reduce as well?
GORBACHEV:	I made clear that these cuts were unilateral steps, undertaken without reference to the Vienna mandate. I have been discussing the range of disarmament, humanitarian and economic questions with the U.S. and our Eastern partners. As for today's meeting, it is not for negotiations; I was invited to New York by the President and Vice President. I hope it will be a useful meeting.
MEDIA:	Is there opposition to the cuts you announced in the Soviet Union?
GORBACHEV:	No.

[A few minutes later, after the media was escorted out, Reagan presented Gorbachev with a commemorative photo of their first meeting in Geneva. "We walked a long way together to clear a path to peace, Geneva 1985 – New York 1988," Reagan inscribed on the photo.]

GORBACHEV:	Those are good words, and I especially appreciate that they are written in your own hand. Thank you, Mr. President.
	I will tell the larger group the same thing later, but I wish to say here as well that I have highly valued our personal rapport, and the fact that in a rather difficult time we were able to begin movement toward a better world.
REAGAN:	As I'm leaving office, I am proud of what we have accomplished together. One reason for all that we have accomplished has always been that we have been direct and open with each other.
GORBACHEV:	Agreed.
REAGAN:	We have accomplished much, but there is still much yet to do. There is a strong foundation for the future. What we have done has been based on the values that have guided our hand, the values we subscribe to in this nation. That commitment to promoting trust and confidence remains. George, would you like to add anything?
BUSH:	No, except that the picture President Reagan gave to you, Mr. General Secretary, was also symbolic of the distance our two countries have come. I do not get to be the President until January 20, but with reference to the three year span since the picture was taken, I would like to think that three years from now there could be another such picture with the same significance. I would like to build on what President Reagan has done, as I told you when we met at the Soviet Embassy, even before the presidential campaign had gotten underway. I will need a little time to review the issues, but what has been accomplished could not be reversed.

Reagan, as Gorbachev must have expected, used his time with Gorbachev to press him on human rights. Now accustomed to Reagan's charges of human rights violations, Gorbachev, without even attempting to conceal his smile, jokingly responded: "Now you can tell the press you raised it again." A minute later, when Reagan handed Gorbachev his final list of names of Soviets he would like Gorbachev to personally help obtain proper emigration papers, Gorbachev, again tried to deflect his counterparts charges. "Perhaps they have already left," Gorbachev told Reagan and Bush.

"I want to remind you of something I said at our first meeting in Geneva," Reagan started his closing remarks. "I am not sure I told the Vice President about it. I told you that we were two men in a room together who had the capability of bringing peace to the world. Now, all these years later, I think it is evident that we had decided to keep the world at peace." "It all began at Geneva," Gorbachev replied.

EPILOGUE

ALTHOUGH Gorbachev hoped to sign a START Treaty at the 1988 Moscow Summit, it took until 1991 for Gorbachev and President George H.W. Bush to finalize the agreement. Once signed, Bush and Gorbachev agreed that each side would have no more than 6,000 nuclear warheads atop a total of 1,600 intercontinental ballistic missiles, sub-launched ballistic missiles, and bombers. Overall, the agreement meant reductions of 25–35 percent of American and Soviet nuclear warheads. Just months before the agreement, Gorbachev at last agreed to delink any START agreement from restrictions on space-based testing for the strategic defense initiative.

That same year, 1991, also marked the end of not only the Gorbachev era, but of the Soviet Union. Gorbachev peacefully stepped-down and dissolved the Soviet Union that December after several Soviet republics, starting in 1988, had declared their independence from the Soviet Union. The Soviet Union officially became Russia, and Boris Yeltsin became the first Russian president.

President Bush and President Yeltsin continued the process of strategic arms negotiations that Gorbachev and Reagan had started. Before President Bush left office in January 1993, Bush and Yeltsin agreed to a START II Treaty. Under START II, intercontinental ballistic missiles with multiple independently targetable reentry vehicles were eliminated, and both Russia and the United States agreed to reduce their strategic nuclear warheads to fewer than 3,500 by the year 2003. START II, however, never entered into force: Russia withdrew from the Treaty after President George W. Bush announced the United States would no longer abide by the 1972 ABM Treaty. President George W. Bush, continuing the Reagan legacy of moving towards defenses against ballistic missiles, abdicated the ABM Treaty so that the United States could test and deploy space-based defenses against ballistic missiles.

Americans and Russians still clamored for further arms control measures. In 2002, Russia and the United States signed the Strategic Offensive Reductions Treaty (SORT). SORT capped the total number of deployed warheads at between 1,700 and 2,200, yet had no verification mechanism, provided that each country could withdraw on three months notice, and did not require the destruction of any nuclear warheads.

President Obama, upon taking office in January 2009, continued the Reagan legacy of arms reductions, and signed the New START Treaty in April 2010. Under New START the United States and Russia are required to further reduce the number of deployed strategic nuclear warheads to 1,550 with only 700 delivery platforms. Most importantly, each side is also permitted to conduct 18 annual on-site inspections. According to the State Department, by October 2012, Russia had reduced their number of delivery systems to well-under 700 (actually down to 491), and similarly had reduced to under 1,500 deployed strategic nuclear warheads. The United States has not kept up with Russian reductions, maintaining 806 deliver systems with 1,722 deployed strategic nuclear warheads.[17]

Twenty-five years after Reagan and Gorbachev last met, the number of deployed strategic American and Russian nuclear warheads is almost 80% fewer than at the height of the Cold War. Most importantly, the number of intermediate range ballistic missiles, the most dangerous class of nuclear weapons due to their short flight time, is still at a global zero. Equally important, the legacy Reagan and Gorbachev left, of building trust through communication, and of working towards the complete elimination of nuclear weapons, lives on through the work of groups like the Nuclear Threat Initiative, the Nuclear Security Project, and the Nuclear Age Peace Foundation.

Reagan and Gorbachev started the process of moving towards the complete elimination of nuclear weapons through a candid and open dialogue and a belief that a nuclear war should never be fought. Their example should be a reminder to current and future leaders of what can be accomplished with just a pen, a few pieces of paper, and the belief that today's problems should not be left for tomorrow's leaders.

---

[17] "New START Treaty Aggregate Numbers of Strategic Offensive Arms," U.S. Department of State, Bureau of Arms Control, Verification, and Compliance, Washington D.C., Oct. 3, 2012. http://www.state.gov/t/avc/rls/198582.htm

NOTES

ALL DOCUMENTS used in this book, unless otherwise noted, were found at the Ronald Reagan Presidential Library (RRPL), in Simi Valley, Calif. All public statements came from the Public Papers of the President of the United States. At the Reagan Library, the National Security Council (NSC) and National Security Planning Group (NSPG) meeting minutes, unless otherwise noted, are located in the collections of the Executive Secretariat, NSC Meetings Files or the Executive Secretariat, NSPG Files.

National Security Decision Directives from the Reagan Administration are also located at the Ronald Reagan Presidential Library in a special collection called National Security Decision Directives.

All letters between Reagan and Gorbachev, unless otherwise noted, were found in the collection of the Executive Secretariat, Head of State Files: USSR. Duplicates of the original letters can also be found online at www.TheReaganFiles.com.

INTRODUCTION

How could he agree to negotiate: A good example of Reagan's thinking on the importance of nuclear weapons to deterrence can be found in the recently declassified transcript of Reagan's Feb. 14, 1984 conversation with British Opposition Leader Neil Kinnock. Reagan told Kinnock at that meeting: "We have had thirty-eight years of peace and, perhaps, the existence of nuclear weaponry has been a contributing factor. ... We are prepared, and the Soviets understand this, to defend our Western sovereignty at any level. ... Fear of the consequences of nuclear war should not be construed to mean that unilateral nuclear disarmament is the proper path to pursue. ... The existence of nuclear weapons has been a key factor in maintaining global stability and preventing war." The complete transcript of this conversation can be found online at: http://www.thereaganfiles.com/memcon_rr__kinnock_21484.pdf. RRPL:

WHSOF: Lehman, Ronald: Files. Folder: British/French Nuclear Forces, 1983-1984 (3). Box 90602.

CHAPTER 1

Feb. 22, 1985:   Letter from Thatcher to Reagan. RRPL: Exec. Sec. NSC: Head of State File. United Kingdom: Prime Minister Thatcher (8590152-8590923). See also Exec. Sec. NSC: European and Soviet Affairs Directorate. Box 90902. Mrs. Thatcher: Visit Feb 85 (1).

March 11, 1985:   Letter from Reagan to Gorbachev. Box 39 (8590272-8590419) (1 of 2).

March 24, 1985:   Letter from Gorbachev to Reagan. Box 39 (8590272-8590419) (1 of 2).

April 30, 1985:   Letter from Reagan to Gorbachev. Box 39 (8590475-8590495).

June 10, 1985:   Letter from Gorbachev to Reagan. Box 40 (8590683-8590713).

June 22, 1985:   Letter from Gorbachev to Reagan. Box 40 (8590683-8590713).

Buchanan's May 27, 1985 memo to Chief of Staff Regan had the subject line, "The Defense Consensus." In his 6th point on why "defense no longer commands the concern, priority, and interest it did in 1980-1981," Buchanan wrote: "In our desire for arms control, the Administration itself has made the argument that the Defense Program has so re-built our armed forces that we can now negotiate from a position of parity with Moscow if not strength – though no such parity exists. We are, in part, victims of our own success. Even many Republicans think we are armed to the teeth." RRPL: WHORM Sub. File FG001 casefile 315674.

Time, September 9, 1985. Gorbachev's full statement was: "Without such an agreement (on SDI) it will not be possible to reach an agreement on the limitation and reduction of nuclear weapons either. The interrelationship between defensive and offensive arms is so obvious as to require no proof. Thus, if the present U.S. position on space weapons is its last word, the Geneva negotiations will lose all sense."

Nov. 21-22, 1985:   The Geneva Summit. Executive Secretariat, NSC System Files (851041 (1)(2)).

CHAPTER 2

Nov. 28, 1985:   Letter from Reagan to Gorbachev. Box 40 (8591143-8591239). The idea to send a handwritten letter originated with Jack Matlock, a senior member of the NSC responsible for Soviet affairs. Matlock, before becoming Ambassador to the Soviet Union in December 1987, wrote many of the initial drafts of letters that Reagan would send to the Soviet leaders after he joined the NSC in July 1983.

Dear Secretary General Gorbachev,

Now that we are both home & facing the task of leading our countries into a more constructive relationship with each other, I wanted to waste no time in giving you some of my initial thoughts on our meetings. Though I will be sending shortly, in a more formal & official manner, a more detailed commentary on our discussions, there are some things I would like to convey very personally & privately.

First, I want you to know that I found our meetings of great value. We had agreed to speak frankly, and we did. As a result, I came away from the meeting with a better understanding of your attitudes. I hope you also understood mine a little better. Obviously there are many things on which we disagree, and disagree very fundamentally. But if I understood you correctly, you too are determined to take steps to see that our nations manage their relations in a peaceful fashion. If this is the case, then this is one point on which we are in total agreement -- and it is after all the most fundamental one of all.

As for our substantive differences, let me offer some thoughts on two of the key ones.

Regarding strategic defense and it's relation to the reduction of offensive nuclear weapons, I was struck by your conviction that the American program is some how designed to secure a strategic advantage -- even to permit a first strike capability. I also noted your concern that research & testing in this area could be a cover for developing & placing offensive weapons in space.

As I told you, neither of these concerns is warranted. But I can understand, as you explained so eloquently, that these are matters which cannot be taken on faith. Both of use must cope with what the other side is doing, & judge the implications for the security of his own country. I do not ask you to take my assurances on faith.

However the truth is that the United States has no intention of using it's strategic defense program to gain any advantage, & there is no development underway to create space based offensive weapons. Our goal is to eliminate any possibility of a first strike from either side. This being the case, we should be able to find a way, in practical terms, to relieve the concerns you have expressed.

For example, could our negotiators, when they resume work in January, discuss frankly & specifically what sort of future developments each of us would find threatening? Neither of us, it seems, wants to see offensive weapons, particularly weapons of mass destruction, deployed in space. Should we not attempt to define what sort of systems have that potential and then try to find verifiable ways to prevent their development?

And can't our negotiators deal more frankly & openly with the question of how to eliminate a first-strike potential on both sides? Your military now has an advantage in this area -- a three to one advantage in warheads that can destroy hardened targets with little warning. That is obviously alarming to us, & explains many of the efforts we are making in our modernization program. You may find perhaps that the U.S. has some advantages in other categories. If so, let's insist that our negotiators face up to these issues & find a way to improve the security of both countries by agreeing on appropriately balanced reductions. If you are as sincere as I am in not seeking to secure or preserve one-sided advantages, we will find a solution to these problems.

Regarding another key issue we discussed, that of regional conflicts, I can assure you that the United States does not believe that the Soviet Union is the cause of all the world's ills. We do believe, however, that your country has exploited and worsened local tensions & conflict by militarizing them and, indeed, intervening directly & indirectly in struggles arising out of local causes. While we both will doubtless continue to support our friends, we must find a way to do so without use of armed force. This is the crux of the point I tried to make.

One of the most significant steps in lowering tension in the world -- & tension in U.S.-Soviet relations -- would be a decision on your part to withdraw your forces from Afghanistan. I gave careful attention to your comments on this issue at Geneva, and am encouraged by your statement that you feel political reconciliation is possible. I want you to know that I am prepared to cooperate in any reasonable way to facilitate such a withdrawal, & that I understand that it must be done in a manner which does not danger Soviet security interests. During our meetings I mentioned one idea which I thought might be helpful & I will welcome any further suggestions you may have.

These are only two of the key issues on our current agenda. I will soon send some thoughts on others. I believe that we should act promptly to build the momentum our meeting initiated.

In Geneva I found our private sessions particularly useful. Both of use have advisors & assistants, but, you know, in the final analysis, the responsibility to preserve peace & increase cooperation is ours. Our people look to us for leadership, and nobody can provide it if we don't. But we wont be very effective leaders unless we can rise above the specific but secondary concerns that preoccupy our respective bureaucracies & give our governments a strong push in the right direction.

So, what I want to say finally is that we should make the most of the time before we meet again to find some specific & significant steps that would give meaning to our commitment to peace & arms reduction. Why not set a goal -- privately, just between the two of us -- to find a practical way to solve critical issues -- the two I have mentioned -- by the time we meet in Washington?

Please convey regards from Nancy & me to Mrs. Gorbacheva. We genuinely enjoyed meeting you in Geneva & are already looking forward to showing you something of our country next year.

Sincerely yours,
Ronald Reagan

Dec. 24, 1985:	Letter from Gorbachev to Reagan and Secretary Shultz's analysis. Box 40 (8591293) and (8690024-8690124).
Feb. 22, 1986:	Letter from Reagan to Gorbachev. Box 40 (8690146-8690267).
April 2, 1986:	Letter from Gorbachev to Reagan. Box 40 (8690146-8690267).
April 11, 1986:	Letter from Reagan to Gorbachev. Box 40 (8690146-8690267).
July 25, 1986:	Letter from Reagan to Gorbachev. Box 40 (8690529).
Oct. 11-12, 1986:	Reykjavik Summit: RRPL: Executive Secretariat, NSC System Files (8690725(1)).

CHAPTER 3

"America has lost": Public Papers of the President of the United States, 5/6/1987.
Sept. 15, 1987:   Letter from Gorbachev to Reagan. Box 41 (8790986-8791196).

Shultz Moscow meetings: Notes from the October 23, 1987 meeting in Moscow are based on a National Security Archive translation of the conversation released by the Gorbachev Foundation and part of Briefing Book No. 238: The INF Treaty and The Washington Summit: 20 Years Later.

| Oct. 30, 1987: | Memo from Shultz to Reagan re: Oct. 30, 1987 letter from Gorbachev to Reagan. Box 41 (8790986-8791196). The letter from Gorbachev to Reagan could not be located. |
| Washington Summit: | RRPL: Executive Secretariat, NSC System Files 8791377. |

CHAPTER 4

NSDD 305 (April 26, 1988), "Objectives at the Moscow Summit," listed the U.S. objectives at the Moscow Summit.
- Stressing the importance of progress in Soviet human rights performance;
- Making maximum practical progress toward an agreement for a fifty percent reduction in U.S. and Soviet strategic nuclear forces;
- Following through on the progress made on the regional agenda, including emphasizing to the Soviets the importance of completing a prompt withdrawal from Afghanistan, reaffirming our objective of a genuinely independent non-aligned Afghanistan in which the Afghan people are free to determine their own future, and actively engaging the Soviets to be helpful in resolving other regional issues on our agenda;

- Consolidating progress and moving forward on bilateral issues, including exchanges and, where warranted, economic relations.

May 29-31, 1988:	Moscow Summit. Executive Secretariat, NSC System Files (8890497, 8890511).
"becoming routine":	RRPL: Exec. Sec. NSC System Files: Memcon, Feb. 22, 1988: "The Secretary's Meeting with Gorbachev Feb. 22." Sys. II 90190.
Sept. 20, 1988:	Letter from Gorbachev to Reagan. Box 41 (8890725-8890750).
Dec. 7, 1988:	Reagan/Gorbachev Meeting at Governors Island, New York. Executive Secretariat, NSC System Files (8890931, 8890944).

ACKNOWLEDGMENTS

Projects like this start and end with the work of all those at the Ronald Reagan Presidential Library. Without their tireless work – from organizing the estimated 50 million pages of documents, to coordinating with the various agencies to get documents declassified, to putting up with my constant demands for more and more information – works like this would not be possible. At the Reagan Library, I would like to especially thank Mike Duggan, Shelly Williams and Cate Sewell, whom I am sure put in more work on my behalf than I will ever know. The same could be said for Diane Barrie, Kelly Barton, Steve Branch, David Bridge, Greg Cumming, Sherrie Fletcher, Lisa Jones, Ira Pemstein, Bruce Scott, Jenny Mandel, Raymond Wilson, Martha Huggins, Kimberlee Lico, Gordon Kaplan and Mike Pinckney. I feel very fortunate to have had the chance to work with each of them.

I have been fortunate to meet and work with several outstanding scholars. Professors Laura Kalman, Tsuyoshi Hasegawa and Salim Yaqub of the University of California Santa Barbara, have all been more supportive than I ever could have imagined. Each have challenged me to be a better writer and historian, and their dedication to the historical profession has served as a model I can only try to emulate.

I am also especially grateful to Timothy Connelly of the National Historical Publications Records Commission for granting me the opportunity to learn about the process of editing historical documents by participating in the 2010 summer editing institute at the University of Wisconsin. There is no question that the editing institute saved me from making many novice editor mistakes.

As with most of my accomplishments in life, nothing much is accomplished without the support of my family. This book would not have been possible but for all of their support. In particular, my father, Joseph Ebin, for whom I've dedicated this book, deserves special recognition. Whatever positive contribution this book makes towards a better understanding of the Reagan years, he deserves as much credit for that as anyone. Thanks Dad!

INDEX

ABM Treaty (Anti-Ballistic Missile Treaty), 20, 21, 28, 29, 30, 47, 50, 71, 75, 92,
      98, 99, 101, 105, 111, 114, 122, 123, 125, 126, 131.
Afghanistan, 5, 6, 15, 18, 19, 24, 32, 44, 45, 55, 66, 70, 73, 106, 135, 137.
Angola, 44, 67.

Baldrige, Howard "Mac" (Secretary of Commerce, 1981-1987), 23, 24, 59, 60, 68,
Bush, George H.W. (Vice President, 1981-1989, President of the United States
      1989-1993), 3, 10, 11, 14, 114, 120, 121, 127, 129.

Cambodia, 44.
Casey, William "Bill" (Director of Central Intelligence, 1981-1987. Mr. Casey also
      served as Reagan's Campaign Manager in 1980. Hours before Mr. Casey
      was scheduled to testify before Congress on his involvement in the Iran-
      Contra Affair (Dec. 1986) he was hospitalized and found to be suffering
      from brain cancer. He died months later in 1987 without ever revealing
      his full involvement in the Iran-Contra affair), 4 (fn).
Chernenko, Konstantin, (General Secretary of the Soviet Union, 1984-1985), 3,4,
      10, 11.
Chernobyl, 86-88, 91.
China, 78, 79, 101.

Daniloff, Nicholas, 98.
Dobrynin, A.F., 43, 48, 81, 84, 85, 86, 87.

Ethiopia, 44.

Flyingdales (Radar station located in Great Britain), 122.
France, 35, 38, 41, 78, 79.

Gates, Robert (Mr. Gates worked in various positions at the CIA throughout the
      Reagan years, including Deputy Director between 1986 and 1989. Gates
      was nominated by President Reagan to succeed Casey in 1987, but his
      involvement in Iran-Contra derailed his nomination. Gates became the
      Director of Central Intelligence in 1991, and then Secretary of Defense in
      2006), 4 (fn).
Geneva Summit, 49-50.
Germany, 14, 15, 17, 18.
Governors Island (Site of Reagan-Gorbachev meeting on Dec. 7, 1988), 126-129.
Great Britain, 30, 38, 41, 78, 79, 120, 123.
Gromyko, Andrei (Foreign Minister of the Soviet Union, 1957-1985; Chairman of
      the Presidium Of the Supreme Soviet, 1985-1988), 110, 14, 20, 23, 33.

ABOUT THE EDITOR

Jason Saltoun-Ebin has been researching the Reagan Administration since 2001. He is the editor of *The Reagan Files* Vol.'s 1 & 2 and the creator of www.TheReaganFiles.com, a freely accessible website devoted to the study of the Reagan administration. The website is now used by scholars all over the world. Mr. Saltoun-Ebin lives in Santa Barbara, Calif., with his wife, attorney Jessica Zetley. He is a graduate of U.C.L.A. (B.A.), the University of Wisconsin Law School (J.D.), and U.C.S.B. (M.A., History). He is also a member of the Bars of California and Wisconsin.

19618137R00089

Made in the USA
Charleston, SC
03 June 2013